HIGH INTENSITY
marketing

Idris Mootee

Editor: Carol Smith
Researcher: Janice Wilson
Cover Graphics: Godfrey Chu

Canadian Cataloging Publication Data

Mootee, Idris

High Intensity Marketing (2nd edition)

Includes bibliographical references and index

ISBN: 0-9731308-2-2

1. Marketing   2. Business Strategy   3.Technology Marketing   4. New Product Marketing

I Title

BF354.S3C6   675 135   C63538

Second edition

10   9   8   7   6   5   4   3   2   1

Printed in Canada

I have enjoyed many blessings in my life, but none greater than my father, A. Mootee. It is with deep gratitude and boundless love that I dedicate this book to him.

Acknowledgements

Many friends and colleagues assisted me in thinking through many of the ideas that fill the pages of this book. They are spread throughout the world. I wish to acknowledge all their contribution and to thank them wholeheartedly for their willingness to read all or parts of the manuscript and give me feedback that was always supportive and helpful. They include Rob Reis, Gerry Greeve, Mathew Ames, Scott Wilkinson, Hans Chung, John Falck, Jerry Fuchs, Larry Weber, Bob Jolls, Janet Gordon, Steve Lerman, Bill Mitchell and Dave Johnson, Paul Hodeges, Sharon Colby, Jon Huggett, Stephen Coley, Dick Shaffer, Jimmy Carson, Jean Murphy, Will Novosedlik, my graphic designer Godfrey Chu and my editor Carol Smith.

My gratitude goes to those special clients and friends—not mutually exclusive groups, I am happy to say—that have been extremely supportive of this effort during the past twelve months, giving me the opportunity to test and apply my thinking within the context of their businesses. They include Bruce Cook, Mark Scoot, Wesley Thompson, George Hammer, Jennifer Luzon, Ron Daniel, Frank Silva and Jackson Bandak. And many amazingly talented individuals at Organic, CBIZ and McKinsey are so numerous that I no doubt will neglect to recognize many deserving people.

And to Pauline, Jaraad and Javier, who continue to make my life a meaningful experience. They make it all worthwhile in the end, and seeing the world through their eyes everyday renew it for me. I am truly blessed, and delighted to be so.

Finally I deeply appreciate the effort, inspiration and enthusiasm of Jules Goddard for writing the foreword in the middle of his vacation during a violent thunderstorm in France. He has always been an inspiring teacher from whom I have truly learned so much.

CONTENTS

Foreword

Ten years ago, McKinsey and Company asked the question, "Is Marketing Dead?" In this timely and radical re-statement of the marketing concept, Idris Mootee shows that marketing, wisely re-interpreted and updated, has never been more vital or more germane.

The Demise of Marketing

It is true that between, say, Theodore Levitt's "Marketing Myopia" of 1960 and CK Prahalad and Gary Hamel's "Expeditionary Marketing and the Corporate Imagination" of 1990, marketing—at least in the way that it was practiced by the majority of companies - could be said to have lost its status, if not its way. Its self-appointed role was no longer that of the intellectual conscience of the business, or the architect of its strategic design, or the builder of its product-market portfolio. Instead, it became a euphemism for selling, but without the tiresome responsibility for a sales-force. It survived merely as the function responsible for all the downstream activities of the business.

It became the investment budget of last resort. Amongst its peer departments - finance, operations, R&D, operations—it operated on the shortest time-horizon. Too often, it became the handmaiden of the advertising agency. Indeed, it acquired the reputation--not entirely unfairly—for being, not the voice of the customer in the boardroom, but a conspiracy against the interests of the customer. In the public mind, "hidden persuasion", to echo Vance Packard's vivid phrase, had become synonymous with what was seen as the black art of marketing. Marketing was assumed by many to be the skill of exploiting human frailty. Gary Hamel caught the mood nicely when he suggested that customer ignorance had become the only profit center of the company.

Indeed, marketing was now suffering from the very disease for which it was invented to be the cure. Of all the buzzwords in the business lexicon, "marketing" is still the one that arouses the most suspicion and the greatest cynicism amongst both consumers and opinion-formers.

Marketing Out-Marketed

In some sense, marketing's role had been usurped by two highly successful, and brilliantly marketed, new disciplines: competitive strategy, and total quality management (TQM). The marketers of these disciplines were, respectively, Michael Porter and W. Edwards Deming. Strategy, as a systematic approach to the art of competing for customers, took over the <u>holistic</u> aspect of marketing (by choosing to define success in terms of "sustainable competitive advantage"), whilst TQM has made its name by operationalizing the <u>customer-centric</u> aspect of marketing (by choosing to define quality as "conformance to customer requirements"). In effect, marketing was dispossessed. All it had left was the day-to-day administration of the marketing-mix.

Back to the Future

It is important to recover the essence of the marketing concept.

The original tenets of marketing—which remain perennially important and true - were that the customer is the only true arbiter of economic value, that shareholders are best served when managers focus on the creation of customer value, that customer knowledge (gained by an artful blend of insight and foresight) is the intellectual foundation of a company's strategy, that the ability to hear the authentic voice of the customer is the quintessential competence of the company, and that everyone in the firm, not simply the marketing department, should feel "personally accountable to the customer".

At the heart of marketing is the well-founded conviction that profit is the corporate reward for knowing things about customers that competitors don't know—for possessing a more accurate predictive model of the customer response function than one's rivals. Competition is a discovery process - with firms vying with each other to model more accurately the preferences and decision processes of customers, and then adapting their offerings to these changing criteria.

In the best companies, as Idris Mootee shows us with his telling examples, marketing practices have evolved to reflect these basic principles ever more faithfully.

	Traditional Marketing	Post-Modern Marketing
The unit of strategy	The company	The end-to-end value chain
The focus of strategy	Stealing share from competitors	Migrating to where the value is
The structure of the organization	Built around products	Built around customers
The focus of the organization	Maximizing the profitability of transactions	Maximizing the life-time value of customers
The measure of strategic performance	Share of the revenues earned by the industry	Share of the wealth created by the value chain

Challenge and Response

These changes of marketing practice have been driven by powerful external forces:

- Hypercompetition, aggravated by businesses themselves adopting increasingly convergent ("me-too") styles of thinking and acting;
- Migration of value, both upstream into the hands of the knowledge creators and brokers (inventors, professional advisors, content providers) and downstream into the hands of consumers and traders (particularly retailers)—with a corresponding hollowing-out of the "middle-ground" (typically manufacturers and assemblers)
- Transparency of markets, driven largely by the Internet and producing greater informational efficiencies
- Assertiveness of customers, well-informed, demanding, discriminating, inquisitive, "unreasonable" and choosy
- Advertising burn-out, with all forms of "adversarial" or mass marketing giving way to "permission-based" and "viral" forms of marketing
- Rise and rise of branding, as customers place increasing value on symbolic, "life-style" or conspicuous consumption, and as suppliers experience a glut of skills in building valuable brands

It is in response to these trends that we see marketing changing:

From: Growing the business by acquiring customers
To: Growing the business by retaining customers

From: Treating the value chain as a supply chain
To: Treating the value chain as a demand chain

From: Analyzing the industry and its barriers to competition.
To: Analyzing the demand chain and the migration of value across the industry

From: Defining marketing by the 4 P's of Jerome McCarthy—product, price, place and promotion
To: Defining marketing by the 4 A's of George Day—arena, advantage, access and activity

From: Organizing the business around product categories
To: Organizing the business around customer groupings

From: Mass marketing to market segments
To: Micro-marketing to markets of one

From: Measuring financial performance
To: Measuring strategic performance

From: Building shareholder value by maximizing profitable transactions
To: Building shareholder value by maximizing customer lifetime value

From: Delivering service
To: Delivering WOW!

From: Thinking of the assets of the firm as the tangibles
To: Thinking of assets as intangibles such as reputation, customer loyalty and brand equity

A 3-Phase Model of Marketing

Looking at the big picture, it seems to me that marketing, as a field of managerial practice aided and abetted by business school theorizing, has moved through 3 phases since 1950—and that this book fleshes out brilliantly the substance of the 3rd and most exciting phase:

Phase One (1950 - 1970)

Marketing as predicting customer response, essentially the skill of modeling the decision processes of buyers so as to understand and serve them better:

- This is the tradition that has its roots in the micro-economic theory of demand, in the concept of consumer sovereignty, and in the theory of markets.
- It recalls Peter Drucker's famous nostrum that the purpose of a business is "to create a customer".
- It finds its most articulate voice in the burgeoning literature on "consumer behavior".
- It is manifested in practices such as marketing research, customer satisfaction surveys, motivational research, observational studies and focus groups.

Phase Two (1970 - 1990)

Marketing as predicting competitive market response, essentially the skill of modeling the strategic choices of competitors so as to pre-empt them, or out-play them, and so beat them:

- The starting point for this approach is the maxim, usually attributed to Al Ries and Jack Trout, that "the problem is not the customer; it is the competitor".

- Positioning and differentiation are the central concepts of this school of marketing, emphasizing the fundamental idea that the necessary, though not sufficient, condition for wealth creation is uniqueness.
- As Porter puts it, "Competitive strategy is about being different. It means deliberately choosing a different set of activities to deliver a unique mix of value".
- In practice, this approach to marketing takes the form of industry and competitor analyses, the search for durable economic advantage, benchmarking, and competitor intelligence.

Phase Three (1990 - the present)

Marketing as out-performing the competitors' predictive models of customer response, essentially the skill of learning about customers faster than rivals and thus being in a better position to exploit first-mover advantages:

- This approach recognizes that, all too often, markets are zero-sum games. Firms win at the expense of their rivals. Shareholder value created by one firm is matched by shareholder value destroyed by others.
- Strictly speaking, there can be only one winning strategy in any competitive market, in the sense that every strategy except one must lose to at least one other strategy.
- The core concept of this school of marketing is organizational learning.
- It draws upon Arie de Geus' observation that the relative speed at which an organization learns is virtually the only remaining sustainable source of competitive advantage in a mature market.
- The clearest evidence of this way of thinking is the widespread use of experimentation, particularly to test hypotheses about customers.

One way of showing what is new and daring about the learning organization is to contrast it with the traditional model of an organization as a control mechanism:

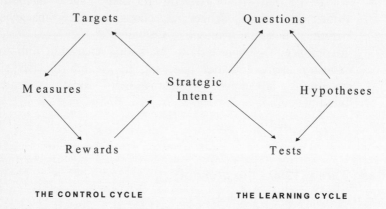

Marketing, in its third phase, aspires to migrate the organization from an exclusive dependence upon command and control as the dominant logic of the marketing strategy process to the rigorous and routine application of the learning cycle.

Three Core Assumptions of Post-Modern Marketing

In this new world of open inquiry—of discovery as the dominant logic of the firm—three bold claims can be made:

Claim One:

In most markets today, the innovations that create the greatest wealth are based on the invention of new business models rather than the application of new technologies

- Take Google, for example. Coming late into the online web-search space in 1998, when most observers were saying that the market was mature, its strategy did not depend upon any breakthrough technologies. Instead, it based its pioneering approach on a new interpretation of what people wanted from a search engine. It read the user differently.

- Google's founders, Sergey Brin and Larry Page, whilst still students at Stanford University, became convinced that what was missing on the web was skilful editing. The role of the editor of any information service is to discriminate - on the behalf of the reader - between what is significant, interesting and useful and what is trivial, mundane and useless.

- What they did was to use the link structure of the web to help them make these editorial distinctions. They interpreted a link from one page to another as a "vote". Thus, the more votes that a page attracts, the more newsworthy the page is deemed to be, and the higher up it appears on the list of search results. The preferences of the market itself are being used, in real time, to shape the product offering.

- This is a hypothesis about consumer behavior. It is not a bet on new technology, though, of course, it depends for its implementation on some clever science. The technology is simply the catalyst. The breakthrough was a marketing insight that currently attracts nearly 30 million unique users a month. It has become one of the most popular and talked-about sites on the web. And it is profitable.

- On the back of this marketing breakthrough, Google has constructed a unique business model. Unlike its rivals and against the grain of the industry, it does not accept banner ads, the hypothesis being that its users resent their presence and therefore remain sublimely indifferent to their appeals. Google nevertheless earns two-thirds of its revenues from advertisers who are given but two choices: to buy discrete text ads or to openly sponsor particular links.

- Google is continuously expanding its product range. Users can search not just web pages and pictures, but also Word documents and discussion-group archives. Also, by simply entering a phone number, the user can access a name, an address, a street map and, in many cases, even a photo of the person.

- Google licenses its search technology to other firms, such as Cisco and Yahoo!, and now sells computers loaded with its own software so that companies can design and run their own customized Google-like search services (Source: "Waiting for Google", The Economist, 23 February 2002)

Claim Two:

The invention of any new business models is ultimately grounded in a unique insight into the needs of customers

- In the case of Google, everything—the corporate strategy, the marketing policies and the operating practices of the company—flows from that single, inspirational, breakthrough conjecture: that search engines need strong editing because, without it, consumers find the signal-to-noise ratio of the web disconcertingly and frustratingly low
- When we talk about differentiation as the "sine qua non" of strategy and marketing, it is not a difference of vision, values and policy that we are primarily concerned with—but a difference of assumptions. Far too rarely do strategic market plans surface (and test) the assumptions (supposedly unique) upon which the entire superstructure of policies processes and practices hangs
- The assumptions that matter most—the ones that ultimately create wealth for the world—are those that capture for the first time some element of the basis on which buyers make choices between the offerings of rival suppliers
- It follows that first-mover advantages attach, not so much to the technological pioneers, as to the "marketing pioneers" who are operating from a brave new set of beliefs about customer tastes and preferences

Claim Three:

Unique insights into consumers are more likely to emerge from market experimentation than the analysis of market data

- Almost all learning—personal as well organizational—is experiential
- Thus, the art of learning is mainly a question of creating experiences that lead to new insights
- Experimentation - or enlightened trial-and-error—is the most economical way of producing such experiences
- In the same vein, Tom Peters sees innovation as "a low odds business—where luck can make all the difference"
- One of the ways in which Peters believes we can manage our own luck is to adopt an experimental mind-set and place lots and lots of small bets. In this way, we are more likely to "bump into the truth" than through the statistical analysis of publicly available data

This is a book that provides a ringing endorsement of the core values of marketing—by taking a rigorously post-modern approach to the subject. Idris Mootee has created a very elegant antidote to McKinsey's pessimistic assumptions about the current and future state of marketing.

Jules Goddard
Fellow, London Business School

Introduction

I have always wanted to write a book that would capture the latest different views of strategic marketing thinking—yet be simple and easy to read. Your time is valuable, so my first goal is to give you a book that you can finish in a plane ride. My second goal is to give you powerful principles that will last a career. Marketing is a critical aspect of business, yet often doesn't receive the attention it deserves. It has become that from the rumblings and soul-searching in the field of marketing that a revolution is brewing. Managers and consultants are discovering that existing models of marketing have reached their limits and some are nearly obsolete in today's fast-paced and high-intensity competitive environment.

Executives who do not have deep marketing experience often have to make critical marketing decisions. 70% of new products and ventures fail due to poor marketing decisions. Though some senior CEOs and executives intuitively understand marketing, many who rose through the ranks in other departments, do not. This book is designed to be a practical reference for both.

Many of the concepts in this book grew out of my work with senior executives over the past twenty years. I felt it was time to begin a dialogue with all types of marketing practitioners about how marketing has changed. This book was written in 2001 and published in 2002 with an original forecast to sell a few thousand copies. It is now being sold in four countries and continues to sell well. The appeal of this book, I believe, is that it puts vocabularies to many of today marketing issues. Seeing the issues externalized in print has a sort of redemptive effect on people who have fallen prey to it in the past. And many marketing executives have told me that this book has become the handbook in their marketing departments.

My involvement with technology-based firms has emphasized the revolutionary impact of emerging technologies on the marketing process. The internet, cognitronics (building an interface between the brain and the computer) genotyping (classifying population segments based on genetics) and biointeractive materials (high technology sensors for living systems) are just some of the developments, which will have a profound impact on marketing. They demand our long-held assumptions be challenged and re-examined as the quiet revolution in marketing unfolds.

Personalization takes on a whole new meaning when you can segment a customer by his or her genetic type. Biointeractive materials dramatically alter everyday products—from a shirt that monitors vital health signs to a TV that measures your level of enjoyment. Is it any wonder that I have had a twenty-year romance with strategic marketing and continue to be intrigued? My hope is that you too, will be fascinated as you learn more about the evolution of marketing theory, concepts and practice.

Up till now, marketing theory has focused on helping companies to see the importance of shifting from product-centric marketing to marketing as an engine of growth. Ted Levitt's classic articles "Marketing Myopia" along with "Success Through Differentiation—of Anything," played an important part in bringing new thinking to both academics and practitioners. Four powerful forces – digitization, globalization, deregulation and miniaturization, shaped and continue to shape very concept of marketing and what it's expected to do.

While many marketing practitioners still consider their discipline to be a series of tools, processes and techniques, academics have attempted to seek legitimacy in the world of scientific research. Marketing research exists, as do specialized postgraduate courses in the field. Management Science is a relatively new field of study. However the use of the term "science" is hotly debated since management is undoubtedly an art as well as a science.

Marketing executives often do not get the respect that they deserve from the rest of the company. This is particularly true in a technology-intensive company. Interestingly, recent research indicates other departments in such companies regard marketing as inferior in terms of strategic thinking, creative problem solving and general competence. In fact they felt their own skills were 50% stronger. A common understanding of "Marketing" includes both the broad company's effort to succeed in the marketplace and the narrow definition of a marketing department's daily activities. In fact most people cannot distinguish between overall business objectives and marketing objectives. The important decisions are made by the sales, engineers, finance and accounting, since these folks carry more weight than the marketing department. It is difficult for marketing to influence strategy, product development, operations, finance and other key business decisions.

Marketers are typically perceived to lack technical expertise and analytical thinking skills. Another perception is that marketers use (or perhaps misuse) "branding" to solve many business problems.

While engineers, computer scientists, and other technical people take well-known logical approaches to problems, marketers are seen as creative thinkers who do not analyze problems methodically. As a result, many non-marketers in a company mistakenly feel that the research done by marketing is not useful. They often believe such work is biased, easily manipulated, and incapable of showing what customers really want. Even worse, they reason, research is useless for a technology product that people don't want until they see it.

In addition, many non-marketing decision-makers feel that marketing does not extend beyond communications. Instead of encouraging marketers to do the rigorous analytical work of segmenting customers, analyzing customer behaviors and positioning products, for instance, they are instead often relegated to the work of communication specialists. Marketing communication is important, but it is only one tactical part of marketing which uses a mix of tools. However tools are not marketing. Marketing is strategy. It is what, when and how a company is organized and mobilized to execute a particular strategy and monitor its performance. It is deciding how and when to use marketing tools. Strategy is the roadmap. It comes first.

Another reason marketers suffer a lack of respect in the organization, is that many of the offending companies have an R&D-driven culture. Such environments often focus intently on creating a cutting-edge technology with benefits that customers must be shown in order to create a need for the product or service.

This is incorrect thinking—firms are supposed to satisfy needs, not create them—that more often than not leads to poor sales. When this happens, marketing unjustifiably shoulders the blame. Marketing of new technologies often requires very different tools and processes that not many MBA schools teach. It is in fact a lot more complicated than other aspects of marketing such as product or brand extensions because it involves more risks and is very different in nature.

Company history harbors a third reason why marketers don't get respect. Old marketing mishaps often become exaggerated in a company. You may hear stories about an infamous marketing mistake that occurred many years back in the company. It could be a product that failed, or a flopped advertising campaign, but it usually happened several years ago and nobody can remember precisely who did it. Nonetheless, it is now a myth of failure worn by marketing. Unfortunately it may profoundly influence non-marketers' views. We

4

often hear people saying we tried that three years ago and we couldn't sell any of those.

The over-romanticized perception of marketing also plays a role in today's problem with marketing. The common perception is that marketing needs to be imaginative, visionary, and people other than marketers cannot understand it. Marketing is out in a pretend world where anything goes. To revitalize a brand, they say they define a new target market, "For the young and urban…." To appear proactive, they intone, "Added values." With the help of their advertising agencies they often set unachievable marketing goals that are doomed to fail right from the beginning. John Murphy, founder of Interbrand, says in an interview, " You must ensure, most importantly, that your brand is differentiated in a meaningful way though not necessarily a massive way." The reality is that what single advertising-given and driven "reason" do people have for choosing between IBM and Dell? United Airlines versus American Airlines? Hertz versus Avis? Wal-Mart versus Kmart? Nokia versus Motorola? Why should some lightweight selling proposition in the form of headlines and visuals change customers' behavior? How different are the brand attributes between Coke and Pepsi? The realist view of marketing is that nearly identical goods cannot be made distinctive by clever copy and striking visuals.

This book is also written to address many problems associated with the marketing of innovative products and technologies. As one of my clients, the CEO of a California-based technology company puts it; " I've read a lot of books available on strategy to help our marketing planning. They are great for providing strategic recommendations for stable markets that contain clear distribution systems and no real threat of predatory invasion from new products and technologies. However, most of the concepts do not apply to our situation – an emerging industry where no markets are certain and threat of obsolescence is always just around the corner."

McCarthy's "4Ps" have appeared in many marketing texts for three decades. Product, promotion, pricing and place (channels) are still considered to be the tactical marketing toolkit available to marketing practitioners. Servicing marketing added the additional

"3Ps" of people, process and physical evidence. For industrial marketing, it is generalized in most introductory marketing texts that the core "4Ps" hold firm.

Compared with most consumer goods, however, industrial marketing has a much stronger customer service aspect to the product proposition: technical advice before a sale, ongoing customer support and aftermarket operations. Marketing channels are often shorter, and dealer networks or direct marketing are heavily used.

The sales force is central, sales promotion is heavily deployed, trade shows and direct marketing are popular, and advertising tends to be more technical and less emotive in nature. Even pricing is different: few industrial buyers adhere to list prices, expecting to negotiate or consider tenders.

On marketing control and implementation, while there are exceptions in some of the more long-standing and mature marketing departments, the sales-oriented culture inherent in most industrial companies has not provided a basis for the required operational controls to ensure the effective implementation of marketing activity.

Marketing activity is more ad hoc, short-term and tactical, rather than on-going brand building or rolling out longer term marketing plan recommendations. Some marketers may perceive these variations between consumer and industrial marketing to be marginal. They are, actually, strikingly different and manifestly alter the manner in which marketing is practiced. But do they make marketing per se take on a different guise and ethos?

In this revised edition, I have added a chapter on luxury goods marketing. This is a very popular subject and with our societies enjoying an unprecedented amount of disposable income, the trend is here to stay. The downscaling or massification of luxury goods has been the single most important marketing phenomenon of modern times.

This book allows you to learn and apply the state-of-the-art marketing thinking and techniques, many of them as taught by top business schools and used by top strategy consulting firms. It helps you demonstrate both sides of marketing, including the one that is truly analytical in nature. For non–marketers, this book provides a common language and will develop your understanding of the process. Consistency is a hallmark of the more scientific and analytical disciplines; if you bring it to your company beyond your marketing department, it'll go a long way. This allows all managers and executives to speak consistently across all issues. I hope this book helps companies to adjust and thrive in a world where marketing is becoming high intensity.

CHAPTER 1

Marketing Revisited

One interesting and important issue that has preoccupied marketing professionals and academics alike for many years is the question of whether marketing be considered as a scientific discipline or an art. As practitioners, the quest for a "science of marketing" is elusive. If science is in part a systematic formulation and arrangement of facts to help promote understanding, then the concept of the marketing mix may be considered a small contribution in the search for a science of marketing.

However if we think of marketing science as involving the observation and classification of facts and the establishment of verifiable laws used by marketers as a guide or formula with assurance of predictable results, then we have not gotten far toward establishing a science of marketing.

Over the last twenty years, marketers have made significant progress in the use of scientific method in tests that measure the results from mixes or parts of mixes. Thereby marketers have been learning how to subject the hypothesis of their marketing mix to empirical check. Here in the first chapter of this book I will begin with the question "what is marketing"? To date, there is not a single definition or approach to undertaking marketing. Here are a few commonly used definitions each with some variations:

The aim of marketing is to make selling superfluous. The aim is to know and understand customer so well that the product or service fits him/her so well that it sells itself (Peter Drucker).

Marketing is the art of finding, developing and profiting from opportunities (Philip Kotler).

Marketing is the management process responsible for identifying, anticipating and satisfying customer requirements profitably (The UK's Chartered Institute of Marketing).

Marketing consists of individual and organizational activities that facilitate and expedite satisfying exchange relationships in a dynamic environment through the creation, servicing, distribution, promotion and pricing of goods, services and ideas (The American Marketing Association).

Marketing is the process of planning and executing the conception, pricing, promotion and distribution of ideas, goods, and services to create exchanges that satisfy individual and organization objectives (The American Marketing Association).

Marketing refers to integrated and coordinated activities of research, product, price, promotion, distribution, customer relations, environmental activity, among others, which are directed both inside and outside of the organization (The Japan Marketing Association).

Marketing is about systematically and thoughtfully coming up with plans and taking actions that get more people to buy more of your product more often so the company makes more money (Sergio Zyman – Former Chief Marketing Officer, Coca-Cola).

Marketing is about selling something to customers that they either don't need or want and convincing them to pay the highest price for it (Regional Sales Manager, used car company).

The marketing concept…integrates marketing into each phase of the business. Thus marketing, through its studies and research, will establish for the engineer, the design and manufacturing person, what the consumer wants in a given product, what price he or she is willing to pay, and where and when it will be wanted (General Electric Annual Report 1952).

There are, however, common themes in most explanations of marketing. The most important are:

- The ability to satisfy customers
- The exchange of product or service for payment
- The need to create a competitive edge over competitors
- The identification of favorable marketing opportunities
- The desire to earn profits or financial surpluses to enable a viable future for the organization
- The utilization of resources are utilized to maximize market position
- The increase of market share in preferred or priority target markets

The number one thing in marketing is: when you try to sell a product or service, first make sure people are willing to buy it, then make sure there is a large enough group of potential customers out there that is willing to pay for it a and make sure nobody can duplicate what you're doing in your space (at least within a certain period of time).

If the "right" opportunities are pursued, the right customers are properly probed and targeted with a "right" marketing proposition designed to give a business an edge over its rivals, it is highly likely that customers will be satisfied, market share will rise in core target markets and profitability will accordingly support a viable future.

Conversely, if a business develops a product or service which fails to reflect customer expectations and needs, is no better than competing offers and takes no account of evolving market conditions, it is unlikely that the future will be prosperous for such an organization.

This applies to both consumer and industrial markets. Definitions of marketing count for little if businesses do not develop a process, culture and set of operational procedures to actually "do" marketing. Traditional marketing textbooks promote an emphasis on a process which hinges on marketing analysis, marketing strategy, and marketing mix tactics and internal marketing controls.

So, is it here where there is common ground: in how marketing is defined and in the marketing process to be "deployed"? Is this how marketing should be explained: a common set of goals put into action through a process of marketing analysis, strategic decision making, formulation of tactical marketing mix programs and operational feedbacks and controls?

Are the apparent differences in buying behavior explanation, competitor understanding, marketing research activity, market segmentation bases, branding, marketing mix ingredients and internal operations, simply examples of marketing academics seeking to exaggerate perhaps only very minor variations in how marketing is perceived and utilized? Are there other, perhaps more fundamental differences between the activities of consumer and industrial marketers not cited in this brief overview? Or are there even more fundamental differences between industrial products and software platform-based products, which very often is a winner-takes-all situation? Is there one way to describe and characterize marketing? Are any differences evident in industrial marketing merely subtle nuances or do they require their own full and proper explanation? Indeed, just what are the principal similarities and differences between "traditional" consumer marketing and business-to-business industrial marketing or technology-based marketing?

The true essence of marketing strategy lies in the relationship of a firm to its external environment. The essence of a market lies in bringing together products and customers. Market strategy is thus the relationship of a firm's product, service and price behavior to its customer environment.

Figure 1-1 Marketing Strategy Linkage

The study of market strategy is not confined to any disciplinary perspective but actually lies at the intersection of three disciplinary areas: corporate strategy, economics and consumer behavior. In strategy terms, it is focused on the firm's strategic intent, its growth requirements and appetite. In economic terms, it is focused on the demand side of strategy. In consumer behavioral terms, it is focused on the customer side of strategy. Because of this focus on the demand side and concern with customer environment, "marketing strategy" has a more specific meaning than "business strategy" or the broader concept of "corporate strategy". Similarly, it has a somewhat different meaning from "competitive strategy", which focuses mainly on the industry structure and competitive dynamics. But over the years this has somewhat changed.

As Regis McKenna puts it "In the years when I was in marketing, we (marketers) would have pricing meetings; we'd go out and set up distribution. Other people are gradually assuming those kinds of things, while software programs are doing more of the functions of managing relationships between partners and customers. Those programs themselves are more and more integrated into a corporate strategy than into a marketing strategy. In fact, I don't think we can tell the difference any more between a corporate strategy and a marketing strategy."

So far there is no framework available to facilitate the interdisciplinary bridge building that successfully combines economic logic and customer behavioral logic. This is drastically different from the logic of industrial economics upon which the competitive strategy literature of the past decade is built. That rigorous logic captured in the supply and demand curves a powerful heuristic for understanding the customer side of strategy, as it is constructed from the building blocks of "utility" (the tangible satisfaction consumers derive from products.) Very few, if any, concepts or frameworks actually peel the onion of "market heterogeneity" to identify the dimensions of each and their implications for market strategy.

The recent and well-documented crisis of confidence in marketing discipline has to a large extent centered around the lack of applicability of marketing theory to marketing practice. Basic tools and tenets of marketing management theory are being doubted and their relevance to modern business questioned.

Many academics and practitioners disparage the Boston Consulting Group Matrix and many see traditional marketing research as inhibiting rather than enhancing the process of innovation in certain industries. Some refer to consumer behavior as a theoretical "black hole", calling for a new paradigm which seeks less to control consumers and more to understand them and accommodate their needs. Many also believe that the marketing concept itself is essentially flawed.

Moreover, there is a general disillusionment with the inability of marketing theory to match corporate realities. Some accuse

13

marketers of not understanding the economics of the business or of different channels of distribution. In their survey, "Marketing at the Crossroads" Price Waterhouse and Cooper identified a large gap between the classical role of profitable marketing and how marketing is practiced by marketing departments within 100 blue chip organizations. They go as far as describing the marketing department as "critically ill" and in need of urgent treatment, warning that winning companies will not have "ivory tower marketers".

The theoretical underpinnings of marketing thought are under an increasing threat and are often perceived as lacking any relevance to the modern business environment. In seeking to redress this balance between marketing theory and marketing practice, it is the marketing concept itself, which receives the most attention from academics. The focus is its development, extension and refinement as, for example, witnessed by the recent proliferation of relationship marketing literature.

The marketing plan, which ideally bridges the gap between theory (the marketing concept) and practice (the functions of marketing), receives much less attention in terms of its basic operability in the hands of the practitioner. Yet, arguably, this is exactly where a firm has the most difficulty. Many executives struggle to translate their marketing plans into an implementation effort.

Here we will examine the role of marketing and its application in helping companies set their growth paths. Is marketing about growth? Or is marketing about creating, communicating and capturing value by discovering growth opportunities? There are a lot of misperceptions about marketing and what it can do for companies. The three most commonly held (and incorrect) views are:

Marketing myth no. 1: Marketing is all about selling

Many people still confuse marketing and selling. Selling is a part of marketing but marketing includes much more than selling. Marketing begins before a company has any products or services to sell. And marketing continues throughout the whole product's lifecycle. It mandates the continued discovery of new ways to create, communicate and capture value. Marketing is not and should not be considered a cost; in fact it is an investment. And like any investment, it must provide a clear idea of how and when it will deliver a return on that investment.

Marketing myth no. 2: Marketing is a department

Another common view is that marketing is just a department. It is true that marketing is organized around a marketing department. But if marketing thinking only happens within this department, I believe the company would stumble badly. Marketing is far too important to be left only to the marketing experts. Progressive companies need to get all their departments to be customer oriented. Marketing must be an integrated part of the whole organization, rather than a specific function. Look at some of the most successful companies today and see who in the organization sets the marketing direction for those companies. More and more, it's the CEO who's becoming the chief marketing officer although they do not usually carry that title.

Marketing myth no. 3: Marketing is all about the marketing mix

Marketing is often being marginalized to just managing the marketing mix and public relations. Many executives believe that marketing is about getting the "big idea" from their agencies and spending money effectively on the advertising and promotional mix, to optimize advertising dollars. It does not matter what products they are marketing, they expect to work with their advertising agencies to come up with big ideas to differentiate their product in the marketplace and win a few advertising awards in the process. Marketing is responsible for generating new products, services, retail formats, new channels, new ways to deliver service, new pricing tactics and most important of all, creating compelling customer experiences.

Marketing is the art and science of finding, developing and profiting from opportunities. In the demand chain, which is the opposite end of the supply chain. It's about using imagination to dream up new products, new services and balancing them with business realities. So what are the main sources of market opportunities and where do they come from? I have used the following list as a starting point and found it to be it is a very effective starting point regardless of what industry you're in:

- Supply a product/service with growing demand and/or in short supply
- Supply an existing product/service in a convenient way
- Supply an existing product/service in an economical way
- Supply an existing product/service in a customized way
- Supply an existing product/service to new customer segments
- Supply an existing product/service to a new geographical market
- Supply an existing product/service under a new brand name or family
- Supply an existing product/service to be used in different applications or settings
- Supply a totally new product/service as replacement product/service
- Supply a totally new product/service in a market that has yet to exist

Often companies find their businesses commoditized, opportunities for growth diminish and sales targets are unmet. For example, a corporation sets a sales goal achievable in three years. It has projected various sources of sales over the three-year period. However its current products and service offerings stop growing as it reaches a certain point in its product life cycle.

Top line sales growth is possible by gaining or buying market share. Another source of top line growth is expanding into new geographic markets and introducing them to new customer segments. An alternative is to launch completely new product families or brands.

Yet all these strategies may not add up to desired corporate top line objectives. The company faces a situation where either they have to reduce sales forecasts or find breakthrough ideas to fill the gap.

What we are dealing with is typical of the situation many companies face, trying to find possible growth paths and new revenue streams. In a well run organization, marketing bears the main responsibility for growing the company's top line. Marketing's main thrust and skill is demand generation and management. Marketing creates and influences the level, timing, and composition of demand in pursuit of the company's objectives. Although traditionally marketers spend most of their time and energy building the level of demand and not enough managing or sustaining the demand (often a function of customer relationship management) under certain unusual circumstances, (such as excessive demand) marketers may reduce or delay demand or change its composition.

One starting point in looking at the different challenges of building or increasing the level of demand consists of four processes: finding customers, getting customers, keeping customers and growing customers.

So what are the most common success factors which turn new ideas into successful and profitable new products? It all comes down to how well a company is prepared to capture and evaluate innovative ideas, and then develop and launch them successfully. Here are some questions to think about:

- Ask each executive to describe the top three opportunities facing their businesses and assess each of those opportunities in terms of potential growth and profit potential.
- Ask each executive to describe three key problems that their customers have and suggest ways to solve those problems.
- Ask each executive to name three things they would never hear from their customers. What opportunities does this suggest?
- Try to map out the customer activity cycle among each major customer segment. What opportunities does each particular point suggest in the customer activity cycle?

- Try to map out the value curve or differentiation index of all your competitors and find out how your products or services are differentiated. What opportunities does this suggest?

It often sounds simple but realizing customers needs and wants and translating this knowledge into products and services is an extremely difficult task. The complexity of this task explains why so many new product launches fail. The contextual understanding of customer needs is easily lost in the product development and market planning process, especially when cost becomes the dominant factor in decision-making.

Figure 1-2 Marketing Point of Exchange

Two Different Views of How Companies and Consumers Think

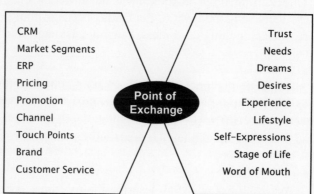

Different disciplines need to work together very closely and success likely depends on the coordinated involvement and knowledge sharing among the multi-disciplinary team. The three main factors that are key to achieving the highest probability of success are:

- The ability to identify new product opportunities beyond product ideas, that solve existing problems, and/or create new customer experiences.
- The ability to get customers involved very early in the process and employ qualitative research tools to deepen consumer understanding within the customer context.
- A heightened contextual understanding of customer needs translated into actionable insights and foresights that define attributes. These attributes serve as a guide in developing and marketing of the products' form and functions. In order for innovative products to be successful, they must have forms and functions that consumers quickly recognize as useful, usable and desirable.
- A true integration of marketing, engineering and design beyond simply putting a multi-disciplinary team together. The team must be supported and managed effectively in an environment where each discipline respects and appreciates the perspective of others.

The identification of innovative product opportunities is the core force that drives growth. A product opportunity exists when there is a gap between what is currently on the market and the possibility that results from emerging patterns and trends. A product that successfully fills a product opportunity gap does so when it meets the conscious and unconscious expectations of consumers and is perceived as useful, usable and desirable.

No one requested Walkmans or MP3s before they were provided and no one expected to be able to do so many things without leaving home before the internet was widely available. Successfully identifying opportunities is both art and science. It requires a constant sweep of a number of factors in four major areas:

- **Product Lifecycle** – These factors focus on the competitive dynamics of a product or technology's lifecycle stage and its market maturity limits.

- **Socio-Economical Trends** – These factors include changes in demographics, psychographics, pycheconometrics (the spending power people have, or expect to have, for purchasing power).
- **Technology Innovation** – These factors focus on direct or imagined results from new scientific discoveries, emerging technology patterns or recent technological innovations.

Investing time and effort periodically scanning these areas has proved rewarding to many companies. The goal is to create products and services by identifying an emerging trend and matching that trend with the right technology, service, design and function.

Figure 1-3 Sources of Marketing Strategy

Marketing is about opening strategic windows into the future

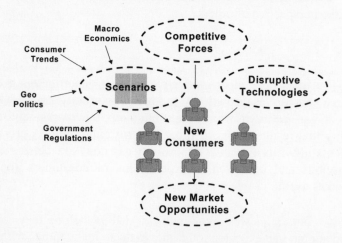

Marketing people should lead this effort, but to capture opportunities continually, a flow of ideas from all across the organization works best. Marketers encourage this flow with a combination of cultural reinforcements, organization designs, feedback loops, and explicit financial and professional incentives. Consequently the whole organization becomes responsible for identifying innovative new market, service or product opportunities.

A good example is Starbucks; it uses strong cultural incentives to drive the identification of opportunities. All company employees are called "partners," signaling a level of responsibility maintained by few companies with sales in the billions of dollars. Anyone who has an idea uses a one-page form to pass it along to the senior executive team—and always gets a response. When the company pursues an idea, its author, regardless of tenure or title, is typically invited to join the launch team as a full-time member.

Consider, for example, the evolution of what eventually became Starbucks' Frappuccino, a cold coffee drink. A front-line manager had the idea in May 1994, and a five-person, top-level team soon gave it a high priority. In June and July 1994, the team developed marketing, packaging, and channel approaches; a joint venture with PepsiCo was in place by August. The manager who originated the proposal was put in charge of a pilot project, and the first-wave rollout started in October 1994. National launch of the product followed in May 1995, and in its first year it accounted for 11% of the company's sales.

Starbucks acts quickly because it has a high-level steering committee that meets every fortnight to rate each new opportunity by two simple criteria: its effect on the company's revenue growth and its impact on the complexity of the company's retail stores. The committee uses a one-page template for each of these ideas and relies on a full-time process manager to ensure that information is presented consistently. Starbucks sets a minimum goal of $4 million in annual revenue for potential ideas but raises or lowers this figure if they make its retail stores more or less complex, respectively.

At Commerce Bancorp, a New Jersey-based bank, a "Kill a Stupid Rule" program rewards employees that that identify a rule that prevents them from wowing customers.

At Home Depot, CEO Arthur M. Blank makes many new business decisions unilaterally, not waiting to build a consensus throughout the organization, but with a robust fact base gathered by a central market analysis group. Moving quickly doesn't necessarily mean making important marketing decisions carelessly.

The process needs to be simple, transparent, fast, and rigorous. It supports entrepreneurialism by ensuring that anyone who generates an idea gets the freedom and resources to pursue it or clear feedback about why it has been denied. The window of opportunity is often small and a product that comes out too early or too late can fail even if the product has potential. For example, Apple introduced Newton, an early PDA with handwriting recognition technology. However, it cost too much and weighed too much to succeed.

When US automakers tried to enter the small car market it was already dominated by well-made fuel-efficient 4-cylinder small automobiles. Saturn encountered modest success, but most US automakers still rely on trucks and SUVs rather than small cars to generate profits.

Du Pont once invested more than $1 billion in digital imaging and publishing. It hoped to capitalize on the emerging imaging technology, but the infrastructure was not yet in place. As Terry Fadem of Du Pont puts it, "the vision was correct, but timing was poor."

We all remember the story of how Western Union turned down the opportunity to buy Alexander Bell's patent on the telephone, which they saw only as an improvement on the telegraph.

The founder of IBM, Thomas Watson, estimated that there was only a market for five computers. This number was the result of estimating the number of calculations performed at that time in the world each year.

Successful innovative products become necessary once they hit the market. Consumers are not even aware that they need a product because they are immersed in the trend. If the company hits the trend when it is just catching on, the innovative product becomes instantly desirable.

The length of a trend combined with product usefulness determines the lifetime of the product. Changes in any one or more of the dynamics produce product opportunity gaps.

Once identified, the next challenge becomes translating these opportunities into development of a new product or the significant modification of an existing product. In both cases, these products are a hybrid combination of a new aesthetic and set of features stemming from the possibilities of innovative technologies and an emerging shift in consumer taste and preferences.

An idea should receive an initial screening to determine its strategic fit in the company or business unit. Three important dimensions should be evaluated: the strategic marketing compatibility of the idea; the strategic technical or operational compatibility; and the commercial feasibility of the new product. The purpose of screening is to eliminate ideas that are not compatible or feasible for the business. Screening is somewhat subjective since the team determines how narrow or wide the screening boundaries are. Some firms develop screening procedures using scoring and rating techniques and these methods are effective only if the team agrees on the relative importance of each screening factor.

Figure 1-4 From Strategy to Tactics

The Anatomy of a Marketing Strategy

The most common problem is determining product-market boundaries and the generic product-market breadth. Ultimately all products and services fit into a generic product-market, concerned with meeting some basic needs. Such a huge category is of limited value in market opportunity analysis and strategy development.

However, a very narrow definition of product market may exclude useful information and ideas about how specific products satisfy the overall generic need.

The important consideration is to try to avoid a generic definition that is either too narrow or too broad. Industry classifications often consist of only one product or product category and are consequently too restrictive. Some considerations in forming product-markets include:

- The number and type of distinct applications a specific product has.
- The number of situations or scenarios encountered by each user.
- The number of alternatives or substitutes users have.

Exploring the definition of product markets alone will often create ideas and is a good starting point. The definition of the product market structure establishes the scope and boundaries for product markets, their size and composition, competition and the needs and wants of their consumers.

Suppose the management of a firm is interested in expanding a mix of laptop and desktop computers. If the present line of products meets a generic need for home and office computing, related product extension includes: printers, monitors, networking devices and storage devices etc. Advantages are gained through common distribution channels, advertising and brand. The process of defining product-market structure begins by identifying the generic need satisfied by the product of interest to management. The best starting point is, and will always be, customer needs.

Another way to approach market expansion is to use market-driving strategies. Instead of adhering to existing product market boundaries and industry structures, companies attempt to change the rules. The strategy here is to avoid competing. And it means getting back to strategy to rediscover the importance of paying painstaking attention to customer needs in search of a superior customer value proposition that is unique and highly beneficial to customers.

Many of today's most successful companies actually drive the market—Dell, Sony, Target, 3M, Nokia, Ikea, Starbucks, Southwest Airlines, eBay and Wal-Mart are all examples of organizations that have revolutionized their respective industries and created huge shareholder value in a unique way.

Wal-Mart is the most notable classic example. They have redefined value to buyers by offering consistently low prices, an acceptable level of service and a well-chosen selection of products.

EBay created one of the world's largest and liquid virtual free markets. It allows people to sell almost anything.

Dell created a whole new way for consumers to customize, order and buy their PCs. Each of these companies is driving its market and being rewarded handsomely for it. Successful market-driving strategies reshape markets, build great brands and define enduring concepts of customer value. They take bigger, yet calculated risks, and once successful, they enjoy a sustainable competitive advantage for a long period of time.

If marketing is all about managing opportunities, how do you balance the three internal voices: the technology voice from the product development team; the customer voice from marketing and sales and the corporate voice from senior management and finance? There is usually divergence between these groups. Many companies set up basic criteria and filters to guide this process. For example:

- The new product or service is ready to launch within the next 24 months

25

- The new product has a market potential of not less than $100 million and a growth rate of not less than 15%
- The new product provides a 30% return on sales and 35% return on investment
- The new product fits with the existing corporate branding
- The new product is capable of achieving product performance or market leadership
- The new product utilizes existing core assets or marketing infrastructures

These criteria can help companies to screen out ideas that are interesting yet poorly suited to an organization and focus on those that best fit corporate vision, business scope and investment criteria. Then within these set of ideas, the company will need to measure the potential profit, potential risks and return of capital invested.

CHAPTER 2

Strategy and Positioning

Research on corporate performance during the last ten years confirms the central principle of textbook marketing strategy; that to be successful over the long term, a firm's products and services must be well "positioned" in the marketplace. However, my own experience shows that many marketing managers are unfamiliar with marketing positioning strategy and associate it only with product level market positioning or marketing communications positioning. Consequently, this chapter aims to de-mystify the concept by outlining the basic components of positioning strategy formulation and isolating the key ingredients that are critical for success. This chapter introduces a framework that allows us to look at the market from a strategic context.

Market Positioning Strategy – The 4Cs

What is positioning strategy? Positioning strategy refers to the choice of target market segment that a business serves and the customers' differentiated advantage that define how it competes with rivals.

This definition shows that a positioning strategy only applies at the specific product and/or service level in a particular market. It should not be confused with the broader concept of "corporate strategy", or with the more specific concepts of strategy as it relates to each element of the marketing mix, such as "promotional" or "pricing" strategy. The above definition also shows that a positioning strategy may be broken down into four inter-related sub-components:

- Customer Targets
- Competitor Targets
- Cost Structure, Channel Choice and
- Competitive Advantage.

Figure 2-1 The Marketing Strategy 4Cs

Positioning strategy formulation demands the ability to picture the marketplace and think creatively about the inter-relationships between these four sub-components. The objective is to find a segment of the market where, by virtue of the company's distinctive strengths, it is able to satisfy customer needs better than (or at least as well as) its competitors. This necessitates a thorough understanding of the strengths, weaknesses, opportunities, and threats profile (SWOT) facing the firm—something that can only be achieved by a dedicated internal company, channel, competitor, and customer market analysis.

Once a positioning plan has been finalized, it is then translated into action by assembling an appropriate marketing mix. These include the 4Ps and the new 4Ps described later in this book. The definition of the traditional 4Ps is: Product, Price, Promotion and Place (distribution), with each "P" comprising a set of decision elements. Together they define the firms' offer to its target market. The mix is tailored so that target customers regard it as superior to competitors' offerings. By reflecting the firm's competitive advantage, the key elements of the mix provide the means to activate the plan. As we move on to discuss the four components of positioning strategy in detail, remember that this is a theoretical exercise, since, as emphasized earlier, they cannot really be considered independently of each other.

Picking the Customer Segments

The selection of customer targets highlights the critical role of market segmentation in the marketing process. Segmentation involves the sub-division of a larger market into distinct subsets of customers, with similar needs and wants and/or responsiveness to marketing offerings. It is a concept based on the following propositions:

- Customers usually differ in some respect.
- Customers are grouped into relatively homogeneous segments in terms of relevant behavior.

- Segmentation enables isolation and targeting of specific markets.

The business logic behind this is simple. If you divide a larger market into smaller segments with different preferences and subsequently adjust your product (or service) to suit the different segments, you reduce the gap between what you offer the market and what it wants and/or needs. This improves your competitive position.

Since most markets contain customers who are either too numerous, widely scattered, or heterogeneous in their buying requirements to be effectively served by one company, your aim is to identify the segments of the market which are most attractive. These choices reflect your customer targets.

In attempting to segment the market, there are many possible criteria. Some common examples include:

- Geographic (where customers reside) local, regional, etc.
- Demographics (who customers are) age, gender, education, income etc.
- Psychographics (what customers think) behavior, attitudes, etc.

There is, however, no one correct approach. You will be most successful if you continually seek new, creative ways to define your market. This effectively requires a continuous process of trial and error. This will help you gain new insights and develop an effective competitive advantage.

Segmentation is possible with virtually any variable as long as it satisfies the following four key requirements:

- Homogeneity within segments. Customers within segments have similar needs, wants and responsiveness to marketing offerings.
- Heterogeneity between segments. Customers between segments have significantly different needs, wants and responsiveness to marketing offerings.

-   Targeting of segments via marketing mix. Segments that can be effectively reached and served.
-   Viability in economic terms. Segments are large or profitable enough to justify the marketing effort being deployed.

Research and my own experience show that the most successful companies are those, which specialize and concentrate on a well-defined market, with a thorough understanding of customer needs. It is this knowledge, which effectively drives all subsequent decisions. The route to success in target market selection is to focus your (limited) resources (time, effort, money) onto a relatively small group of customers whose needs you can meet most effectively.

Selecting Competitive Targets

Successful marketing is all about aiming to satisfy customer needs and wants and how they behave better than the competition. You must identify and select customer targets to enable the firm to exploit some competitive edge in the marketplace. This necessitates a careful analysis of the competition. Evaluate your competitors in the light of your own company's relative strengths and weaknesses and your ability to compete through superior skills or resources.

Research shows that the most successful companies are those which, if possible, avoid head-on competition altogether by offering something different. The challenge for businesses already serving the market is to cope with the changes that threaten the positioning of the company. In other words, find a strategic window and open that window when the fit between the critical success factors in a market and the distinctive competencies of a business serving that market is at an optimum.

Emerging technology may create or destroy opportunities in one market or allow you to simply modify existing products to fit in with the needs of a new customer segment with high growth potential.

Technological control is not, however, necessarily a critical success factor. Keniche Ohmae, a renowned strategist, argues that the most effective shortcut to a competitive leadership position is an early concentration of major resources, in a single strategically significant function in order to excel in that area, and consolidate the lead in the other functions.

Understanding Channel Choice and Cost Structure

As a marketing strategist, you must understand the overall cost structure and channel dynamics of the business thoroughly. It is important to analyze channel choices and options as part of the strategic process and vital to have a deep understanding of the relative cost standing of your business, as well as flexibility and the ability to transfer professional experience to a variety of corporate sectors.

Channel options are often ignored and most companies seldom confront the choices of channel mix. For example, whether to appoint an exclusive dealer network versus pushing for intense distribution or another intermediary is strategic; it should not simply be determined by the characteristics of the product or service. Very often, distribution strengths play a distinctive role in reinforcing superior product performance and maintaining a strong market position in the end-user market. In the case of information products, channel options may be the defining elements of the product.

Passive acceptance of existing channel choices is increasingly risky for two big reasons: Companies in all industries face increasingly high sales costs with little evidence of productivity to offset these costs and customers continue to put high demand on manufacturers that permit direct communication and information flow, forcing companies to reconsider traditional channels.

Cost relates almost directly to scale and scope. Until recently scale and scope was always guided by two rules of thumb: bigger is better, and keep as many activities as possible under one roof to retain control and maximize revenues. Adherence to these ideas lead to extensive vertical integration and continuously striving for scale and mass marketing with a strong volume orientation. Many quality and control issues are solved by supply chain technologies. The issue of scale is still very valid as there are always benefits of specialization.

A strategist must understand the cost relationships between scale and scope as it has huge implications to the overall marketing strategy. In the foreseeable future, strategy will continue be dominated by the use of technology and scale-economics as basis of sustainable competitive advantage.

Identifying Competitive Advantage

You must also develop a competitive advantage that distinguishes your company's offer from those of your competitors in the segment. In other words, decide how the business is going to compete in the marketplace. The aim is to make the offer as unique as possible to customers, so they are less likely to switch brands for minor price advantages.

When developing a competitive advantage, always base it on something of value to the customer (e.g. superior service, extraordinary human factor design or high level of customization etc.) and not price alone. It is critical that your competitive advantage is to some extent "sustainable". In other words, it should exploit distinct competencies of the company that competitors find hard to copy or at least take considerable time and resources to duplicate. Although this is becoming more and more difficult nowadays, competitive advantage can be created out of any of your company's strengths or "distinctive competencies or capabilities" relative to your competition. Managers of successful companies always have a crystal clear understanding of their competitive advantage and use it as a blueprint for all strategy and marketing decision-making. Some prefer to call these "distinctive competencies" strategic assets.

An asset loses its value not only if competitors can easily duplicate it but also if another asset can easily substitute for it. To assess your assets you must ask questions such as: Do firms without this strategic asset face a big competitive disadvantage? How many other competitors also possess this asset? Is it possible to substitute other assets for this one? Are there any emerging technologies or killer applications that take away the value of our strategic assets? You must identify such strategic assets and understand them well enough so that they become part of the building blocks of your strategies. You cannot afford to stop and celebrate your current advantages. Be paranoid about competitors and move aggressively to defend your positions. As important as a strong defensive strategy might be, it only delays erosion. All market strategy has a life limits and this means continuously innovating to build new sources of competitive advantage.

Michael Hay and Peter Williamson, who developed the strategic staircase as a managerial tool for companies to build strategy assets and capabilities as part of the strategy development, have proposed five principles to maximize its effectiveness:

- The strategic objectives are defined clearly, concisely, and in terms that are motivating.
- Skills and capabilities are developed in a deliberate and sequential manner. The precise order in which capabilities are developed is specified and explained to employees.
- Difficult choices on what to invest in and what not to invest in are made.
- Timetables are agreed upon for the building of the different steps in the staircase.
- Measures by which progress on the initiatives will be judged are clearly defined and used.

Making the First Strategic Move

Organizations typically make two types of mistakes. They get too caught up in product innovation, particularly developing new technologies and new products, or get too obsessed with competing in market share in any given product market. Although these are not exactly bad things—after all business is all about innovation and getting the largest market share - both could be damaging if the focus is on the wrong indicator of success.

Product innovation often leads to a strong internal focus on fixating technical development and lack consideration to commercialization and marketability. As a result, many technologically innovative firms fail to bring their products successfully to the market. Competing for market share often creates a mentality that leads to believe the game is all about share points, not customer value creation. It drives incremental thinking and encourages managers to try to gain market share at any expense. It is crucial for any company to be able to look at one's market posture before deciding your move and this is a critical step that is often being ignored. Every organization should have a market strategy (philosophy) that guides the planning and implementation of all its marketing activities. This philosophy then becomes a corporate identity about target markets and how the company will serve them.

Marketing is about strategic entry into a market with the intent of subsequent market domination. It is the difference between having a piece of the pie, the whole pie or even making it a bigger pie.

The first important starting point is to decide on where and how to compete. This positioning needs to be supported by other positioning strategies at the product marketing level and serves as the basis of the overall strategic thrust. Consistency and congruity of other marketing activities, based on a unified vision and shared understanding of the overall strategy are essential to superior marketing performance.

This tool allows the strategy team to choose the battlefield and determine the manner or the mode of attack. The strategic matrix has been arbitrarily divided into quadrants and each quadrant associates with a prototype strategy:

-     Evolutionary play, mass markets;
-     Evolutionary play, niche markets;

-       Revolutionary play, niche markets;
-       Revolutionary play, mass markets.

Evolutionary Play Mass Market

Unless one already dominates the market, a company competing in this quadrant simply competes within the rules and structure of the industry. Basically the market leader sets the market definition, standards, features, pricing and customer service level. New entrants seldom succeed in displacing market leaders. Yet many organizations persist in a "follower" strategy, not recognizing that they have other strategic options. Companies in this quadrant can usually only achieve mediocre performance. There may be regulatory or geographic barriers to entry or the market is considered too small or unattractive by market leaders.

Figure 2-2 Strategic Competitive Postures

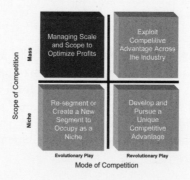

Evolutionary Play Niche Market

Firms in this quadrant follow a shredder strategy and seek to gain some competitive advantages selectively by focusing their resources and energy on a market niche or niches in which they offer something unique to those particular customer segments. They can choose to do that by focusing on unique product design, advanced technology or unmatched customer service. These segments are often ignored or underserved by the market leader or economics does not allow the bigger players to serve them profitably.

In most cases, companies competing within this quadrant avoid direct head-on competition and so the chance to get into a price-cutting competitive situation is minimized. Moreover, companies can operate profitably over a long period of time simply by investing and defending their turf. The barriers to entry include geographic factors, regulatory factors, economies of scale and technical standards that result in customer lock-ins. However, if the niche grows to become too attractive and the company success becomes conspicuous, big players invade this niche using their scale-based advantages. Companies must determine whether their intent is to occupy and defend this market and continuously monitor changes that could result in lowered barriers to entry for their large competitors.

Figure 2-3 Strategic Competitive Postures

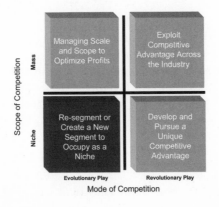

Revolutionary Play Niche Market

This is still where most competitive battles for innovative products and technologies are fought today. Bets are usually big and battles are short, but they come one right after another. Since each axis of the game board is a continuum, the location of the dividing lines between new game and old game are constantly moving and the lines are arbitrary. True new game strategies can be distinguished by the following:

- They seek to change the rules of the game through strategic innovation rather than adaptation.
- They often exploit factors that are not regarded as competitively important and defy conventional wisdom of the marketplace.
- They do not seek to optimize the business system but rather to change the industry dynamics and shape industry structures.
- Sometimes their strategies may appear to be illogical and therefore allow them to escape the radar screen of large players.

If you decide to compete with a new revolutionary play strategy you must determine whether you want to test it with a few small selective markets. Beyond redefining one or more segments, selective revolutionary play strategies can sometimes create new segments that previously did not exist or could not be reached. Most large markets evolve from niche markets. That's because niche marketing teaches many important lessons about customers.

Intel entered the personal computer (PC) business a few years before Apple started to market its first computer. The company advertised the early version of the personal computer in Scientific America and showed a junior high school student using the product. Intel's marketing research, however, revealed that the market was too small for personal hobby computer and abandoned its business plan of launching personal computers for home and hobby uses. As it

38

turned out, many of the early users of personal computers were in education and small business. An early forecast for the personal computer market in 1978 projected that the PC market would reach $2 billion in 1985. The PC market exceeded $25 billion.

Figure 2-4 Strategic Competitive Postures

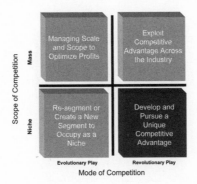

Revolutionary Play Mass Market

This quadrant is where the risks are the highest and so is the potential return. A company that takes this approach expects to change the entire marketplace or industry for complete market dominance. This is usually resource intensive and requires tremendous market power. Such power stems from killer applications, control of industry standards, dominant distribution channel, powerful brands, and proprietary or patented products that have no close substitutes. Companies that have real market power include Wal-Mart, Intel and Microsoft. Such a firm can basically change the competitive rules overnight and modify the requirements of the market to match their strengths and further raise the barriers to entry.

By being able to rewrite the rules, companies in this quadrant achieve a sustainable competitive advantage. Often the competitive advantage achieved by a revolutionary play strategy is more sustainable than evolutionary play strategies. Companies that have successfully created shareholder value by moving from Revolutionary Play Niche Market to Revolutionary Play Mass Market include Wal-Mart, Ikea, Southwest, Amazon, eBay and Edward Jones. Some companies like Wal-Mart take more than 30 years to move to the mass-market quadrant and some take only a few years.

Figure 2-5 Strategic Competitive Postures

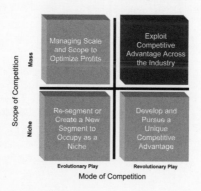

Strategy is dynamic in nature. It has a time limit and no strategy works forever. The line between evolutionary and revolutionary play strategies is constantly shifting and the speed depends on the pace of competitive innovation.

Once the innovator has rewritten the rules of the game, others are forced to follow. The new game inevitably becomes an old game. When this happens, the innovator reaps big rewards, as it becomes the market leader. Then others who want to change rules again challenge the dominant position. An innovator needs to look for new ideas and opportunities to redefine the rules to its advantage or simply play the scale game to maximize return until the next game. It is a constant battle in the marketplace between the innovators or attackers trying to make money by changing the order of things, and defenders protecting their cash flow. Looking at corporate success for the last 30 years we can see pattern and principles that caused events to unfold as they did. In most cases companies with new ideas and approaches, not entrenched large ones, collectively have the innovators' advantage.

Innovation is always risky, but not innovating is even riskier. The biggest barrier to innovation is a host of mental models—the core assumptions that are never questioned. These mental models translate into deep beliefs that everyone in the organization takes for granted. The most dominant of such beliefs is what business you are in and what markets that you serve. Sometimes referred to as "business definition", this determines how your company is going to play the game.

The strategy matrix introduced here helps determine this. The results become an effective guide to action, and expand to include other components of the marketing strategy. Unfortunately, many companies have not made a conscious decision about how they are going to play the game. This means in turn that many moves that they make are influenced by a strategy they are largely unaware of.

CHAPTER 3

Product Level Positioning

Laurel Cutler, a lifestyle futurist, is recognized as one of the most powerful women in the advertising industry because she has the knack of understanding consumer lifestyles and where they are heading. In the mid 70s she saw consumers becoming more savvy, more value-oriented, smarter shoppers, based on greater access to information. She notes that these consumers look for value when they buy in the most expensive as well as the cheapest stores.

Their search is for distinctive merchandise that helps answer the question "Who am I?" This shift to a "me" orientation and the greater focus on independence and individuality that follows confirms her acumen. The key to the future, according to Cutler, is to "help customers find something to hang onto, to sink roots into. One hundred percent quality, real service, unique design, style." In short, help them express their identities.

For marketers, aesthetics is not a matter of esoteric art theory. It is a way we communicate through the senses, the art of creating reactions without words. It is a way to make the world around us special. Aesthetics is not just only for design-centric items but also for techno-centric products. Computers, network servers, home audio systems, speakers, TVs, digital cameras, cell phones, for example, all used to look pretty much the same. Now they, too, can be special.

The product–level positioning approach is about this. This matrix integrates design, technology and service delivery. Together they comprise the total customer experience. Successful integration of all three results in the creation of breakthrough products with strong "meaningful" differentiation in the marketplace, perceived by consumers as high value. In contrast to traditional product features-and-benefits based positioning, this matrix helps you focus on the total customer experiences that occur as a result of encountering, undergoing, or living through situations. Design, technology and service components work together to trigger stimulations to the senses, the heart, and the mind. They connect the company and the brand to the customer's lifestyle, and place individual customer actions and the purchase occasion in a broader social context. The experiences provide sensory, cognitive, behavioral, emotional and relational values that significantly enhance functional values.

Although it is possible to achieve great success by focusing on one dimension (usually these companies are perceived as innovators from a design or technology standpoint) I believe the biggest opportunity in value creation is the result of the relentless pursuit of all three, particularly in today's hyper-competitive environment. Traditional marketing takes an engineering-driven, rational, analytical view of customers, products and competitions. This view was developed in response to the industrial age and early stages of the consumer age, not the information, branding and communications revolution that we face globally today.

Traditional marketing cannot explain the success of Volkswagen's New Beetle, Apple's iMac, iPod, Starbucks, Sony VAIO computers, Herman Miller's Aeron or Nokia phones. These products are not just about the superiority of functional features. In contrast, experiential marketing focuses on the customer experience. The incorporation of ergonomics, style, communications, visual/verbal identity, signage, product presence, co-branding, spatial environments, electronic media and most of all, service delivery are part of a marketing campaign used to create these experiences. Products are no longer bundles of functional characteristics but a means to provide and enhance customer experiences.

Figure 3-1 Product Level Positioning Matrix - Chair

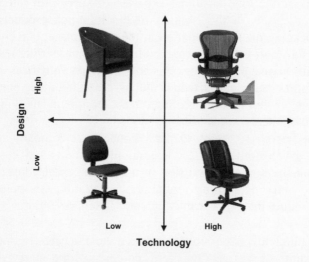

Let us define design, technology and service delivery. These terms can mean different things. I am using them in a specific way. Here, design refers to the form and the sensory elements that communicate the desired aesthetic and human factors of a product or service.

The form must respond to consumers' expectations. It needs to create an identity for the product as well as reflect on the identity of the user. It is the measure of how well a product relates to the lifestyle of the users who are the core intended market. The functional and ergonomic issues must also complement the basic aesthetics.

Technology refers to the core function that drives the product, the interaction of different engineering components and the methods and material used. The core functionality can be mechanical, electrical, digital or any combination of these. Interaction with core technology requires as little as a touch of a button. In some cases operation is through a set of physical switches or commands. The choice of material and manufacturing is appropriate to the projected cost. Fulfill the requirements of internal components, and complement the style requirements of the product.

Service Delivery is a defined set of customer related activities performed as part of or in support of a product. No product really needs to be a commodity. The trick is to know what services your customers want, provide them and then charge more. Companies that sell soap, perfume, candy bars, and other consumer products are expert at "decommoditizing" them: finding and capturing the value of intangible benefits and building strong brand names that provide differentiation in the minds of consumers.

Many companies that sell products such as bulk chemicals, paper, and steel to businesses are unsophisticated in these matters. Burdened by corporate cultures that emphasize operations and sales over marketing, these companies constantly strive to churn out more and more product, more and more cheaply and to sell as much of it as possible at the market price. Viewing themselves as commodity producers, they are particularly likely to overlook the nonfunctional features of their products—delivery speeds, after-sales service, and so on.

As a result, such companies leave large amounts of money on the table. They are far better off taking a page from the playbooks of marketing-oriented businesses and embracing them. Sometimes buyers care not only about the price of a product but also about the way it is sold, the services that accompany it, and the nature of their relationship with the seller.

If manufacturers take that approach, they would find themselves thinking about their customer base not as they have traditionally segmented it—large and small, living in cities or suburbs, income level and so forth—but as composed of businesses that want (and are willing to pay for) quite different things. This would in turn help them focus on the segments whose business they can win and retain most profitably: the segments seeking product or service attributes that correspond to their strengths.

In a recent example, Rubbermaid, a company that makes containers such as seal-n-save food storage containers etc. is undergoing a massive turnaround effort. The new CEO is rejuvenating the company via repositioning. The new products are not only functional but also driven by design savvy that has marked recent successful product launches such as iMac and the Volkswagen Beetle. The key according to CEO Joseph Galli Jr. is to infuse the products with a sense of newness.

The positioning tool here demonstrates how different products in the same category are located in a 3D matrix with design, technology and service delivery. Each dimension has cost implications that are offset by offering products at higher prices, increasing sales or increasing margin through higher brand power. Customers are always willing to pay more for products if they feel that those products deliver their promises, fulfill their needs and give them unique experiences.

With the growing sophistication of the next generation of consumers, products that lack integration of design, technology and service delivery are not perceived by consumers as valuable. While segments of customers are always price sensitive, all customers have some purchases that are based on lifestyle compatibility and association. The higher the lifestyle compatibility, the less important a role price plays in determining purchase. Marketing is the differentiation of anything and these are the three core dimensions that form the basis of differentiation.

46

In the old era of mass marketing, purchasing tended to be consistent along taste and economic lines. In this era of "mass-personalization" and "de-massification," purchasing is highly variable. A person can live in a small house in a suburb but drive a BMW or Mercedes. Another person may own an expensive high-end home entertainment system including a plasma TV but buy all his clothes from discount outlets. The point is no one buys everything to match or project his or her lifestyle or reflect his or her identity, however almost everyone buys something that does.

The historical integration of design, technology and service delivery has been slow and particular in developing economies and mainstream North American consumers. Historically, the two primary factors that people valued most were cost and emerging technology. For the last 100 years or so, companies and inventors developed new products based primarily on technological innovations or particular manufacturing processes. For the period between 1850 and 1950, hand-made production methods were changed to mechanical and then developed into electromechanical processes. The challenge was to make things in large quantities at the lowest cost.

Big compromises were made in terms of customizability and quality, partly due to the North American "use-and-discard" economy. The continued emphasis of cost over craft contributed little to North American industries and consequently European products led the way. Aesthetics and human factors were always secondary or even non-existent in the development of North American products with the exception of a few firms such as Herman Miller and Apple computers. Marketers did not have any input and their sole function was to push the products down the value chain. The common term "form always follow function" was applied not just to industrial or professional products, but also across the board to all industries from furniture to consumer electronics and automobiles.

The last 30 years marked the development of many technological innovations that translated into mass adoption of appliances or machines for both home and commercial use. Major development milestones in this period include Eastman Kodak's introduction of the first compact camera, Apple's personal computer,

Sony's introduction of Walkman and DVD, Nintendo's introduction of the GameBoy and N64 video game console as well as other innovations such as the cellular phone, digital video cassette recorder, digital camera, fax machine, personal digital assistant, plasma TV, microwave oven and GPS system etc.

Technology during the industrial revolution made products and services available to the emerging industrial urban middle class at an unprecedented rate. All the products mentioned above gradually became more available and affordable over the years. But the idea of "form follows function" has always been the dominant logic behind these developments.

The technological advances of mass production met the growing appetite for mass consumption as the standard of living increased and arrival of the "yuppie" generation created the need for more products and services. Generation "Xers" and "Yers" continued to create demand for products that offer more than basic functions. Some described this as the "service" economy. Many early versions of products resulting from new technological advances were ugly. Efficiency preceded design. Television only started to look attractive a few years ago when Sony introduced a simple design, which almost everyone followed. Bang & Olufsen's design was too expensive to manufacture on a mass scale. TV suddenly started to look smart recently with the introduction of flat-screen new technology. What about the PC? It has always been a bulky eyesore. Apple built an incredibly loyal customer base entirely upon design, from the first Macintosh to the first iMac and to the latest flat-screen iMac and iPod. Most PC manufacturers still apply the logic of "form follows function" with a few exceptions.

One such exception is Sony. The Japanese consumer electronics giant entered the notebook computer business with a highly successful VAIO line based on stylish and modern design. The electronics giant re-entered the U.S. desktop market three years ago after a fizzled entry in the mid-1990s. Rather than focus on price, Sony chose to concentrate on industrial design and on integrating software into its PCs for managing music libraries or recording TV programs. Despite its higher than average-selling price, Sony gained market share in the retail market, putting it in fourth place behind Hewlett-Packard, Compaq and Emachines even with limited channel and marketing support.

Up to now, technology and cost alone has driven the development of products for consumers. It took more than 50 years for consumers to demand more of new products. Traditionally only high end products for the upper class were well designed and supported by reasonable services and support, not mass market products.

In the 1950s, US companies such as IBM and Westinghouse developed brand programs that merged their state-of-the-art products with emerging international style. Graphic corporate and product identities, product designs, workplace designs and architecture were all subjected to rigorous guidelines under the direction of external corporate identity consultants.

By the mid 1970s consumer patterns began to change. Companies began losing business to new entrants who stressed not only technology, but also design and service delivery. The first Macintosh computer combined both form and function and was an instant success. The mouse was an easy-to-use and revolutionary feature that added further to the user-friendly interface. Steve Jobs was a true believer of integrating form and function. Apple's success took IBM completely by surprise. Xerox lost their dominant position in the photocopier market to Japanese competitors who compete on both form and function as well as service delivery. Xerox finally got back its market position by backing up its products with excellent services.

As competition grew in consumer and certain industrial markets, companies started to apply human factors and visual design to differentiate products and build strong brands. This became increasingly important as functional components became standardized commodities. The new competitive battleground is integration of design, technology and service delivery. Every consumer searches for a sense of integrity and their own version of value, quality and service that helps fulfill their lives. Consumers not only seek for well-made, easy to use products that match their needs, they require good support. Increasingly consumers want products that reflect their inspiration and make a personal statement. Unfortunately, traditional marketing offers little guidance to capitalize on the emerging experiential economy. I believe innovative new products need to bring all three elements together. We are already seeing a lot them. Coffee lovers can now buy a Capresso smart coffee and expresso machine that is not only cool-looking but incorporates a built-in programmable computer, a water care filtering system, and professional conical burr grinder with six settings. It brews a cup in less than a minute and even warms up your mug. You can customize your java for desired strength and temperature and the machine even does auto rinsing.

When Mercedes launches the legendary Maybach—an 83 year old brand $300,000 super luxury car that has been packed with high-tech gadgets such as Mercedes electronic collision detectors and highly customized styling, they spare no expense in giving buyers the personal service they deserve. At the touch of a button, owners will be able to reach a personal "liaison manager" to handle problems around the clock.

Figure 3-2 Product Level Positioning Matrix – High End Home Audio

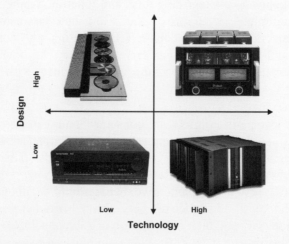

Positioning: Design Vs. Technology

We can now look at how products differ in their use of design vs. technology. The four quadrants illustrated here represent key differences in the level of design and technology if incorporated into the product. The upper right quadrant is the one to be in if your goal is to be a leader in the marketplace and you want to maximize your profit. Success in this quadrant will depend on how ready your industry is to adopt new products as well as the industry and product lifecycle. On the upper right quadrant, balance is achieved through the use of design, technology and service delivery. These products maximize features, functions, ergonomics, lifestyle and personal gratification. We will now examine each of these quadrants in more detail.

Lower Left: Low Use of Design, Technology and Service Delivery.

Most products in this category are typically generic, designed and manufactured with established technologies and very basic styling and packaging. Usually they have little lifestyle impact or do little in terms of reflecting their consumer lifestyles. In short, people who purchase products in this quadrant look for function at the lowest cost with minimal service. The purchase experience is purely transactional and products in this quadrant establish the baseline of the product category.

Such products are usually materially and manufacturing driven, using the minimal amount of raw material, packaging and minimal service to keep cost per unit low and make a profit. Volume-driven with little or no customization, this is classic mass marketing. You can apply the traditional marketing 4Ps to push these products into the market. It is an approach that still works for commodity products. It is a scale game and it works provided you understand the limitations. Almost 70% of all Stock Keeping Units (SKUs) available in large category killers such as Staples, Costco or Home Depot belong to this quadrant. They include printing paper, pencils, paper clips, nails, light bulbs, box files, cables etc. Within this quadrant, consumers seek value in the mass marketing sense. For companies, the products are made as cheaply as possible and profit is made by sheer volume, as margin is razor-thin.

Figure 3-3 Product Level Positioning Matrix

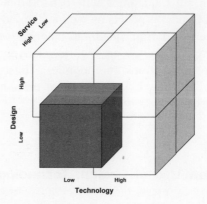

Lower Right: Low Use of Design, High Use of Technology and Service Delivery

Products in this quadrant are driven mostly by technology and often need to be supported by a reasonable amount of service. They maximize the use and applications of the technology and its capability and generally ignore lifestyle and ergonomic needs. They are usually newly launched "solution" products; offer strong technological differentiation and claim to have some sort of leadership or advantage over competitors' products or serve in a certain niche. Profit in this quadrant is based on technological innovation as a result of intensive research and development efforts or knowledge accumulated by serving a professional market. A small segment of customers are always willing to pay premium prices for products in this quadrant. However, the margin and early success usually does not continue these small segments. This is well described as "Crossing the Chasm" by Geoffrey Moore in his best selling book under the same name.

Figure 3-4 Product Level Positioning Matrix

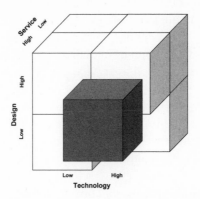

Real value creation only occurs when products hit critical mass. There are hundreds of examples of companies who were considered product leaders but lost their market share to the inferior technology of well designed and marketed products. Examples include Barco (distinct leading makers of LCD projectors), Hewlett-Packard, a once very successful scientific instrument, medical equipment and computer company, Revox, a former leader in audio recording equipment and Leica, a prestige German camera and scientific optical equipment maker.

In order to reach mass markets these firms must move up to the upper right quadrant. Making that transition is not easy. It is not just about repositioning the product lines or having a product or brand identity. However, with few exceptions products do not remain in that quadrant and stay successfully.

The VCR is a classic case of a tech-driven product with more and more features, yet with a horrendous interface. Still no one attempts to improve it. It is almost unusable and yet still no one attempts to do anything since it will soon be obsolete.

Upper Left: High Use of Design, Low Use of Technology and Service Delivery

Products in this quadrant are driven only by style. Companies in this quadrant explore the boundary of aesthetic experimentation and usually fail in the application of human factors (ergonomics) and core technology (features) as well as service delivery.

Design often emphasizes look and feel yet may often lack usability and practicality. However, they push the boundaries of design to the limit and see this as a point of departure from conventional and mainstream products.

Profit happens only when consumer sees products as designer pieces. Such products may be over-designed and consumers realize this cosmetic approach does not provide real user benefits and cannot sustain justification for its high price. This strategy is suitable for a brand extension line or for firms simply looking for niche markets that are willing to sacrifice usability for design and personal expression.

Figure 3-5 Product Level Positioning Matrix

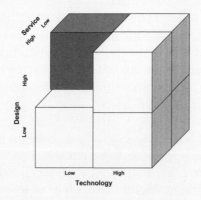

Right Left: High Use of Design, Technology and Service Delivery.

This quadrant contains products that integrate form and function and back them with excellent customer service. This drives long-term (not merely temporary) success. Here features, human engineering, advanced technology, lifestyle reflections, personal expressions all come together to create desirable yet technologically competent products that are differentiated from competitors in a manner that is difficult to replicable.

We will see more and more form combined with function in future new products. Sony teamed up with Target to deliver an exclusive line of smart looking home gadgets that includes everything from a shower radio to a universal remote. Prices lower than Sony customers would expect to pay. Target also teamed with designer Philippe Starck to come up with a range of products from chairs to kettles. These products are affordable partly due to Target's scale driven low cost retail and distribution infrastructure.

One other example is Panasonic's new B-Tube in-car entertainment system. This outlandish looking stereo system with a champagne gold fascia is designed to be as conspicuous as possible. In addition of having four-valve amplification, it has a glowing B tube in the center and a pair of big VU meters. It plays all kinds of CDs as well as MP3s.

At first, service offerings simply replaced products. For example, people increasingly went out for meals instead of buying food to cook at home. More recently, a new type of value-added service has emerged—the "experience"—for which consumers are prepared to pay more.

In the travel industry, the majority of mid-market holiday-makers can now buy a complete package of travel and entertainment from Club Med, while niche operators deliver experiences tailored to the desires of numerous smaller, more defined segments.

Figure 3-6 Product Level Positioning Matrix

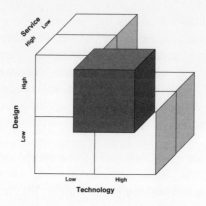

Experience providers like these not only spare consumers the trouble of assembling a package from separate components but also ensure that the experience has a consistent theme and quality throughout. This trend towards delivering a complete experience is highly visible in many other industries. Examples include automobiles (which can now be leased in packages that include maintenance and service) and fast moving consumer goods (Haagen-Dazs Cafes in Asia and Europe) to telecommunications (managed service offerings) and luxury goods (Louis Vuitton, Tiffany, Hermes).

In the past, most consumer goods companies sought to grow by pursuing product-related opportunities alone. Detergent companies, for example, conscious of consumer interest in convenience, launched a series of product innovations, such as combined detergent and fabric softener in single-dose tablets. Such innovations seek to get more people to spend more money on the product.

Expanding reach through new channels, such as launderettes, aims to increase the number of occasions on which the brand is consumed. Stretching the brand to accommodate new products, Mr.

Proper wipes for example, does both. However all these familiar approaches to growth rely heavily on product innovation.

Recently, however, many fast moving consumer goods (FMCG) companies have begun experimenting with the service side. Unilever, for example, has launched "myhome", a comprehensive cleaning experience. Consumers avoid shopping for cleaning materials, having to clean their homes or washing clothes by paying Unilever to do everything for them, using trusted Unilever products. Here, a consumer goods company seeks to add value in an existing service category— domestic cleaning, 'Myhome' builds on Unilever's established reputation in domestic cleaning. products to offer trustworthiness in domestic cleaning services, a fragmented industry where trust is usually in short supply.

Similarly, Nestlé's "Nespresso" business goes well beyond selling coffee beans. It aims to provide customers with everything they need to enjoy café-quality espresso in the home: custom-designed espresso machines; premium coffee in sealed capsules; "Nespresso"-branded accessories (from cups and spoons to sugar and chocolate); and access to advice, through membership of the "Nespresso Club".

Nike has announced its intention to redefine itself as the company that will "make you a champion", partly by selling electronic health and fitness monitoring devices along with sports equipment, and helping customers to interpret the data generated. The company provides fitness advice to anyone who logs on to 'Nike.com'. Lego has introduced a portfolio of new learning and play concepts for children to enjoy within a Lego-branded environment, including Lego activity centers in shopping malls and Lego-endorsed educational materials for primary school teachers.

Most of these new businesses are still embryonic, and it is too early to judge their success. But they all share a common theme - a broader definition of consumer benefit beyond products that rely heavily on service delivery. Opportunities to redefine consumer benefits like this fall into three broad categories

- Combining a set of goods and services (at present available separately) to make it easy for consumers to enjoy an experience they really want—such as a truly great cup of espresso at home.
- Improving an existing experience through service innovation that is at present delivered by fragmented or under-performing service providers—house cleaning, for example.
- Creating a totally new level of service experience that consumers never experienced before with the help of emerging technologies.

A common fear is that broadening offerings to consumers to include greater service results in a labor-intensive, low-margin, low-return business. However, analysis suggests the contrary.

In France, for example, consumer service companies earn an average EBITDA margin of 16.5% on sales, compared with 12.1% for the Fast Moving Consumer Goods sector. Returns on invested capital are similar, at 9% and 10.9% respectively.

Operators who deliver a high-quality "experience" as opposed to average "services" command premium prices and generate even higher returns than the average cited. A prime example—returning to the coffee market—is Starbucks, which has pursued this opportunity and created a business of similar size in terms of sales to Folgers – the U.S. leader in packaged coffee—but with consistently higher margins.

The line between products and services has eroded and what once appeared to be a rigid polarity is now a hybrid: the "servicization" of products and "productization" of services. As products and services merge, it is critical for marketers to understand what the hybrid is not.

The service delivery component is not about providing efficient service repair or a 10-minute wait limit on a 1-800 support line. What customers want most is a satisfying and memorable experience. It is the service that is integral to the whole product offering. It is not based on any event; it is the process of continuously delivering customer value through enhanced services. The product is the service and the service is the product. The product and service is the experience. There is no doubt that for any product-based company the transition to a "consumer experience company" is not without challenges.

After organizations create a whole new level of experience for target customers they brand it accordingly. The starting point is the market and what it values. In the automotive industry, General Motors created a "branded experience" with Saturn. Its slogan is "A different kind of car; a different kind of company". GM's complete engineering of the customer experience and a Saturn dealer neatly summarized the brand:

"We knew from the beginning that, if Saturn was to succeed, we'd have to do more than just sell a good car. We'd also have to change the way the cars are sold, the way the people who sell cars are perceived, and the way the customers feel about the experience of shopping for a car".

Within five years of the launch, Saturn was the No. 2 car in retail sales with a retention rate of 61%.

Branding a customer experience requires careful design and planning. Yet companies still need to experiment rather than place big bets. For ambitious companies, the prize is huge—the opportunity to compete in a market many times larger than their existing one, with more profit potential than their current businesses, and which fits closely with their capabilities. Mapping your products and your competitors on this map not only allows you to understand the scope of your competition but also allows you to ask what you need to move there. What and how follow. The process is usually deep and intricate.

Many companies make the mistakes of combining various elements of the marketing mix without reference to a positioning strategy and hope that advertising positioning alone will work magic. It is rather like trying to make sense of a 1000-piece jigsaw puzzle of a satellite photo of the earth without the benefit of the picture on the box!

Only once you have built up a picture of the marketplace and know precisely how you will compete, can the marketing mix work to your best advantage. Coming up with the "right" positioning strategy is not something that "just happens". Positioning strategy formulation is an extremely time-consuming and complicated task. It demands a good deal of marketing research and analysis to understand the marketplace fully, and because there are no rules and no right way or wrong way to interpret it. Ries and Trout sum up the essence of the challenge: Marketing is a totally intellectual war in which you try to outmaneuver your competitors on a battleground that no one has ever seen .... It can only be imagined in the mind.

There are, however, a few common sense principles to bear in mind, and the purpose of this chapter is to filter them out, and show how they can be applied. They are summarized in the following seven-point checklist:

-   Is it based on a comprehensive situation analysis of your company, your competitors and your market?
-   Is it, as far as possible, built around your company's particular strengths?
-   Does it precisely define your customer targets with a thorough understanding of their requirements?
-   Does it precisely define your competitor targets, reflecting a coherent competitive strategy?
-   Does it precisely define a sustainable competitive advantage?
-   Is it actionable—translating into a distinctive marketing mix?

Formulating a marketing positioning strategy demands analytical ability, patience, creativity, imagination and sheer instinct —but above all it demands wisdom. Sometimes the best positioning strategy is not to enter the market at all!

Once you are in the market, the next big challenge is developing the right value propositions to reflect market positioning. No one company is good at everything. Companies all have limited resources (with a few exceptions such as Microsoft, which basically has the resources to compete in almost every adjacent product category and beyond) and must decide where to concentrate them. Choosing to be good at something also means that you may not be as good in other things. Strategy is about choosing what one is good at, what one is not good at—and what one needs to learn in order to be competitive. So what are the broad positioning alternatives? Harvard Professor Michael Porter, in his Competitive Advantage, proposed three broad generic alternatives: product differentiator, niche market provider or the low cost provider. He suggested that any companies that try to compete in all three without being superior in any way would lose out to firms that are superior in one way. The worse position is in the middle. Companies simply cannot organize themselves in a way to compete since each positioning would require a very different operations strategy and culture to support them. Recently a handful of companies use technologies to compete in all three competitive arenas. One example is Amazon.com, whose business scope expands beyond books and CDs and they built their distribution infrastructure so that they are the lowest cost provider. This is achieved by leveraging scale and personalization technologies, working towards becoming niche providers in every sense. In short, they are competing in scope, scale and niche. But this is an extremely uncommon case.

In marketing, unlike strategy, you need to exceed broad generic positioning in order to express concrete product benefits, reasons and expressive values for consumers to buy. Equally critical you provide them with a reason not to buy from your competitors. As a starting point, you can draw ideas from such possibilities as:

- Best quality
- Best product performance
- Best reliability
- Best aesthetics or design
- Best value for money or least expensive
- Best functional features

- Most prestigious and exclusive
- Most advanced technologies
- Most fun
- Most convenient
- Most simple and easiest to use
- Most personalized
- Most innovative

Figure 3-7 Product Level Positioning

You may choose to have secondary positioning to support the primary ones. Triple positioning, applied differently in different geographic or user markets is also possible. In developing specific positioning, consider the following possible sources:

- **Product attribute positioning**: The company positions itself on its product features

- **User benefits positioning**: The company positions itself on the basis of user benefits
- **Application positioning**: The company positions its products as the best in performing certain functions
- **Competitive positioning**: The company position itself as the best alternative to a marketing leading competitor.
- **User positioning**: The company positions its products in terms of target user group and/or perceived user status.
- **Category positioning**: The company positions its products as the category leader or creator of that market category.
- **Value positioning**: The company positions its products with the best price/quality equation.

Surprisingly many companies today have no idea of what type of positioning strategy they are using or where the competitive arenas are. It is important to avoid the following:

- **Irrelevant positioning**: company positions its products to claim a benefit that no one cares about.
- **Doubtful positioning**: Company positions its products with a distinct benefit no one believes that they can actually deliver.
- **Confused positioning**: Company positions its products to have too many benefits and becomes too confusing for the consumer.
- **Inconsistent positioning**: Company changes its product positioning too often and therefore loses credibility.
- **Over-positioning**: Company positions its product with too much differentiation so that consumers cannot associate the product with its category or its application at all.
- **Under-positioning**: Company fails to project a strong enough positioning to articulate its unique benefits.

CHAPTER 4

The Marketing Mix

Most recent debates about the nature of trends in marketing theory point towards a shift in marketing philosophy. The last five years are likely to be remembered as the time when the long-heralded "Information Age" finally became a reality and gave birth to the network economy. Against a background of technology proliferation and wildly fluctuating, unforeseen changes, the usefulness of contemporary marketing itself is frequently brought into question.

This modern economy is the result of three influential factors: the exponential decrease in the price of computing (Moore's Law); the exponential increase in value of the network due to the number of users (Metcalfe's Law); and the exponential expansion of bandwidth (Gilder's law). The combination of these three influences necessitates updating the classic marketing textbooks.

The marketing frameworks taught at business schools are still rooted in the industrial age, when the function of marketing was to help push products down the value chain. A one-way flow of goods and services from producer to customer was presumed, and the only way to understand the customer was for the producer to initiate market research.

Now, however, the power has shifted. It is no longer a one-way street. As Professor Philip Kotler notes in his book, "There is little doubt that markets and marketing will operate on quite different principles in the early years of the twenty-first century. The successor to the Industrial Economy—the Information Economy—will penetrate and change almost every aspect of daily life."

This chapter proposes a model of strategic marketing in the information economy that extends beyond industrial-age thinking. It proposes a more dynamic view of marketing strategy that incorporates rich externalities, places a strong emphasis on relationships, and incorporates the dynamic nature of markets central to the new economic environment.

The Need for Change

What is strategic marketing in a world that has been transformed overnight by the internet, wireless and other information and networking technologies? What are the strategic frameworks we can use to analyze this new business landscape of change?

The creation of a universal network has drastically altered the economics of information flow and the nature of its availability.

Conventional assumptions are reversed. Information asymmetry is replaced by information democracy. Marketer-initiated exchanges are replaced by customer-initiated exchanges. Product-centric thinking is replaced by activity-centric thinking. And the network allows markets to be reconfigured and realigned by third party intermediaries.

These developments clearly demand a fundamental shift in the formulation of marketing strategy. Marketing thinking must evolve from a functional view based on the simple exchange of product for payment (the 4Ps—product, price, placement, and promotion), to a view of the market as a dynamic system.

In order to determine what strategies will work in these new conditions, it is necessary to re-examine the fundamental definitions of marketing and market-driven organizations.

Figure 4-1 Marketing 4Ps

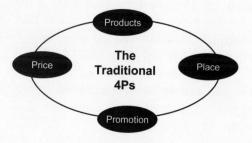

As the above diagram illustrates, marketing promotes the expectation of a mutually advantageous exchange. This exchange is consummated if both parties believe that it is in their best interest to do so. Each expects to be better off after the transaction than before. Thus the "functional" model of marketing rests upon two optimistic assumptions about human behavior: first, that each party to the transaction is able to rationally assess the costs and benefits, and second, that each party is free to participate in the transaction. It simply remains for the market-driven organization to find a need and fill it.

In the industrial economy, that need was fulfilled by tangible products, and in the service economy by intangible services. The information economy has changed that. Value exchanges are now based on payment for information. Consequently, the amount, availability, latency and direction of that information drives the way these exchanges are structured. Industrial-age exchanges assume that information is asymmetrical and scarce. A useful example is the traditional investment brokerage, which is founded on the assumption that those who have large amounts of capital to invest will get the best information. Likewise, consumers' desire for assistance is impeded by the assumption that information is in short supply and comes at a cost.

But what if information is totally or almost free and of very high quality? In today's economy, information is abundant; what is scarce is our ability to process it. An example of this transformation is seen in the telecom industry. In traditional telecom, network architecture was founded on the assumption that bandwidth was scarce, bits were "dumb", and the network had to be "smart" to use bandwidth effectively.

In the new telecom network, bandwidth is abundant, bits are smart and the network doesn't need to be.

If we use this as a metaphor for the entire economy, it can be said that we are developing "Smart Markets", in which the ability to process information, not the information itself, is the scarce resource. Under these conditions, the balance of power shifts towards the customer. Information is abundant, ubiquitous and free. The information-rich regime empowers customers with new capabilities, and enlightened marketers must adopt new assumptions about how to come to terms with customer-initiated marketing (or "reverse marketing").

From Metaphor to Paradigm

A paradigm shift often begins with a metaphorical shift. In the industrial age marketing was like a machine. The marketer cranked up the machine by spending more marketing or promotional dollars, driving both market share and sales volume upward.

In the network economy, marketing is more akin to gardening. Like the gardener, the marketer works with elements that are beyond control. The weather, for instance, is a chaotic system. Prediction is difficult, making it necessary to manage the garden in a much more fluid way. Likewise, in the information economy, the response of the customer is fluid. To create the right environment and provide the right ingredients for businesses to grow, marketers must be skilled at seeding, feeding, and weeding customer relationships.

Marketing has gone through evolutionary changes in the last thirty years. The first generation of marketing took a functional view, dominated by the 4P's: Product, Pricing, Promotion and Placement. This view focused on decisions marketers made, but did not articulate how these choices linked together to form an end-to-end process.

The next generation of marketing took a process or "value chain" view: understanding, realizing, communicating, and delivering value. Like the functional view that preceded it, the process view is inadequately linear and static. The processes are considered individually, and interactions among the processes are not addressed.

The fluid conditions of the information economy demand that the process view evolve into a systemic view, in which marketing strategy is the act of managing a system of interrelated business processes that are inherently dynamic, nonlinear, and cross-functional.

Some familiar elements of strategic marketing are becoming obsolete. What, after all, is the "market share" of a company that can't specify what industry it is in? What good is the "experience curve" when a company jumps from one area of competence to another every few months? What good is trend extrapolation when

68

the past is a poor predictor? What faith we can put into market research when the most important segment may not yet exist? What does strategic marketing mean when uncertainty and rapid change have become the norm?

The watershed at which marketing finds itself can be compared to the difference between Newtonian and Einsteinian physics. Newton's laws of motion work fine in everyday life. However, the assumptions of Newtonian mechanics break down when objects are accelerated close to the speed of light. We need to invoke Einstein's theories of relativity under these conditions.

Figure 4-2 Consumer Experience

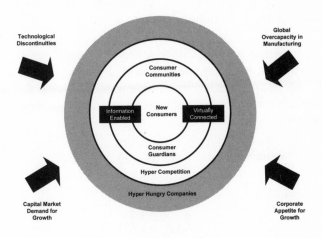

In the network economy, businesses evolved and changed at speeds where traditional marketing frameworks are of limited relevance. These warp-speed conditions demand a shift from a static and firm-centric perspective to a dynamic and network-centric perspective. As was mentioned earlier, the information economy is fueled by three inter-related phenomena: digitization of information, technological innovations and network explosions. Collectively these may reduce transaction costs, increase the reach of information, and collapse response time. Such changes are profound and rapid enough to challenge the classical view of marketing and the marketer in modern organizations. To remain relevant and strategic, you need to move beyond tinkering incrementally with traditional marketing concepts. You must question the most fundamental assumptions.

The New Marketing 4 P's

In the network economy, strategic marketing plays a different role. It is now "relationship-driven", "network-centered"', "technology-enabled" and "information-intensive". Marketing collected feedback from the customer and packaged or re-packaged the product in response. The function requires an integrator, knitting together all business functions in a cohesive response to the dynamic nature of personalized customer relationships.

Marketing in the information economy must adopt a perspective that is encompassing and strategic, not narrow and tactical. By way of illustrating this new way of thinking, the following analytical model supplement the traditional marketing 4Ps. I call them The New 4Ps.

Figure 4-3 Marketing New 4Ps

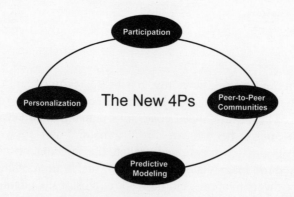

70

Participation

In 1991, John Seely Brown, then Director of Xerox Palo Alto Research Center, referred to customers as the "ultimate partner". Involving and allowing customers to pick and choose from a large number of product and service combinations has always been a remarkably attractive value proposition. Consumers get a reasonably priced, tailor-made product reflecting their personal choice of specific features, styles, functions and level of service.

Although not a new concept, the success enjoyed by Dell and other high tech companies that build products to order has become the envy of manufacturers of all industries. Ford and GM have launched full-fledged built-to-order experiments for customers in certain cities. Nike allows customers to customize with a personal pair of Nike online. Barbie dolls are ordered with custom choice of hair, ethnicity, style, dress and accessories.

Levi's Original Spin allows you to create your very own custom-fit Levi's. Walk into a Levi's store in San Francisco and use a computer to choose the model, fabric, even the type of fly you prefer. After a full body scan, an associate takes a few measurements. The custom fit Levi's arrive in two weeks. The cost: $70.

P&G has enjoyed considerable success from its online build-to-order venture Reflect.com. It allows women to build their own beauty products. Fill out a questionnaire and describe what you want in a lipstick or shampoo. Reflect.com has risen above a virtual bloodbath in many online retail sectors, including beauty products, and in later 2001 launched a design-your-own perfume section. While almost all dot.coms were laying off employees, Reflect was adding staff. Based on customer input, Reflect.com recently revamped its skin care moisturizer line and the result was exploding sales, growing 500% in six weeks. P&G corporate web site each month invites online consumers to sample and give feedback on new prototype products. If the product gets rave reviews, P&G might then decide to bring it to retail stores. It is also an excellent way for them to prove to retailers that there is demand for these new products.

Examples are also found outside the consumer product and computers industries. Green Mountain Energy Resources in South Burlington, Vt., sells electricity through mass customization. It offers customized electricity from sources that pollute less than conventional coal plants. In California, the company offers mixes of geothermal- and hydroelectric power. In the future, it will offer wind- and solar-generated electricity.

Andersen Corp. in Bayport, Minn., which sells windows for homes, says it uses a PC-based customization tool to help customers wade through the millions of possible window and design combinations. Now widely used by the company's distributors, they take orders directly from consumers. Other companies including fashion and sporting goods can leverage the internet as a customer participation and customization tool. It addresses consumers' demand for individualism (personalization), sizing (fit) and aesthetic (style) and provides compelling customer value.

As the internet matures and fades into the background, it becomes an information utility that is part of any business marketing technology infrastructure. Participation from customers allows companies to reverse-engineer the desires of their customers beyond what traditional research can do.

One recent example is Ikea, a large global home furnishing company. They asked their customers to participate not only in their product design, but also their store design. In search of a more compelling shopping experience, with the help of consultants, the firm asked customers to come up with a design for the Chicago store to fulfill their wish list of requirements. The result was a three story octagonal-shaped building, with a central atrium that serves as the shoppers' home base. From there they can locate the eight departments on each floor. A survey reported that 85% of people coming to the store rated the shopping experience as excellent or very good.

This participation concept is also being extended beyond products to the brand. When the founder of Burton, the worldwide cult snowboard brand, was asked about his customers, he replied that they felt they owned the brand. His customers, mostly teenagers and young adults, want to get involved and take an active part in creating and building the Burton legend.

Another example is Levis, who let their customers pick the Super Bowl ad they wanted to see. Levi's launched SuperVote to let consumers vote on the Web for the ad, out of three choices, that Levis aired during the NFL championship. The effort, a partnership with Yahoo, makes Levi's the first advertiser to turn the high-stakes choice of advertising over to its customers. It is also a bid to gain an edge in the pre-game hype by Super Bowl advertisers.

Personalization

The word personalization has moved beyond the web and has a new meaning. It moves into a multi-channel and cross-category environment. The word was once commonly and casually used for first generation personalization technologies that were limited in both functionality and application. They failed to deliver on promises as many struggled to use them to craft the rules that determine content and how to make the technology work. Today we have moved closer to leveraging rich customer knowledge to actively tailored content, marketing messages and most importantly, products and services that deliver real customer benefits.

You can use unified profiles and matching logic to ensure smart interactions with customers across all touch points. Garden.com uses profiles to warn customers when a plant they are about to buy won't grow in their climate.

Car Points provides maintenance suggestions and recall alerts. Cross channel personalization is key. Banks are able to use unified customer profiles and logic to facilitate smart interactions with customers across all channels from the Web to ATM and Interactive Voice Response systems on the phone.

A company called Savage Beast developed a technology that allows customers to enter a song title and a database of songs and music finds songs with similar tunes and rhythms. Since most people base their music preferences on melodies that they already know this is a powerful tool for music lovers. Imagine this combined with audio recognition technologies. A consumer can walk into a music store or call in by phone and hum a few lines and he will be offered selection music to be downloaded or put onto a CD or DVD. This also makes the music buying experience more fun, since people often do not know the name of groups and base purchase decision on hearing a song once or twice on the radio. With this technology customers can easily find what they want.

As information devices mature into consumer appliances companies provide personalized mass products. A leading manufacturer of foam products has created a revolutionary new material, originally developed by NASA to use as mattress to increase the comfort of Astronauts during space journeys. The material is called visco-elastic foam, and it is the key to the Memory Foam Mattress topper. The open-celled construction of Memory Foam creates a mattress with a memory. It automatically senses your body weight and temperature, and then it responds by molding to your body's exact shape and position. It distributes your weight and reduces stress on your body's pressure points: the shoulders, hips and legs.

When you lie down on this amazing material, the heat-and pressure-sensitive foam react to your body's weight and temperature, so it molds to your exact body shape. This means that whether you sleep on your back, stomach or side, your weight is evenly distributed and your spine remains in a neutral position. Other surfaces support your body only at the shoulders, hips and legs.

LG is a Korean—based company with a vision of a new class of "smart" appliances that communicate with each other through a "Living Network System". This is a personalized digital home assistant. The Living Network System utilizes the internet refrigerator as the "residential gateway" to the home—allowing appliances to interact via a digital home network.

They envision everything in the house connected through the refrigerator since it's the only appliance which remains on 24 hours a day. Their vision is to create appliances that go beyond a simple mechanical function, like heating or cooking food. Instead, these next-generation appliances collect recipes, prepare meals and keep pantries stocked—tasks that require intelligence. LG's refrigerator is now available in U.S.; the 26-cubic-foot refrigerator features a high-quality 15.1-inch TFT-LCD and its own LAN port to enable internet surfing and shopping, as well as two-way videophone calls with friends and family. It is also used for watching TV, listening to music and e-mailing messages to friends. A digital camera mounted on top of the LCD enables video messages and digital still photos to be created, exchanged and printed.

The refrigerator makes extensive use of touch screens, a simplified graphics user interface, electronic pen and voice messaging for a user-friendly experience. You can check real-time price information on groceries; obtain tips on food, nutrition and recipes; be reminded of scheduled events; be informed when to change the refrigerator's filter, and learn cooking methods for products stored inside. You can use the internet refrigerator as a TV, radio, Web appliance, videophone, bulletin board, calendar and digital camera.

The internet microwave has an embedded modem and LCD panel, so you can download recipes from the internet, automatically set appropriate cooking directions and "sense" when food or beverages are perfectly heated. By downloading information from the internet, the microwave will be able to cook food automatically. There is also a function for consumers to bookmark major food-related sites for the latest information and cooking trends. The microwave allows a direct connection to grocery stores so you can order groceries from connected retailers in the comfort of your own kitchen.

The company also plans to launch the internet Turbo Drum Washer that can continually download new wash-cycle programs from the internet for different kinds of clothing. It features a 4.2-inch LCD window and 4Mbit flash memory. Unlike conventional washing machines, which operate only according to factory settings, the Turbo

Drum actually tailors the washing program to your preference with the help of the internet. The machine's washing method can also be programmed, thereby creating a personalized wash each time. Eventually, the machine will allow control and monitoring of its operations from a remote location.

Even broadcast advertisers with roots in mass marketing are playing fields of the future. Consumers already watch what they want, when they want and this trend will continue. Middlemen like TiVo, ReplayTV and Wink, though vigilant regarding privacy, have precise information on viewer income levels, spending habits, viewing habits, interests and preferences. Instead of a single extinction-level event, think more in terms of an unstoppable evolutionary process. The coming changes are nevertheless profound.

The Digital Video Recorders (DVRs) of today are capable of recording about 30 hours of programming. That will mushroom to hundreds of hours within the next two to four years. They are clunky, separate appliances that will be incorporated into televisions or satellite/cable receivers.

ReplayTV has been acquired by SONICBlue; TiVo has begun revamping its business model and paring its work force; and upping the stakes further, Microsoft is now in the game (Ultimate). Whichever companies or business models win out, a majority of viewers will embrace DVR and ITV technology. They will be watching even more of what they want, when they want. Events like the Super Bowl, current programming like the election coverage, and even high-quality television shows will still exist and thrive in real time. But overall, time slots will mean less, and competition for viewer interest will grow exponentially.

The broadcast world may evolve to where the most popular shows, rock videos and movies, once broadcast, are recorded (by DVR) or downloaded using Video On-Demand (VOD) and viewed more frequently than ever before. They're already popular—now they're convenient too. More and more programming may never even be broadcast in the traditional sense—it may exist as a VOD file only.

The least popular shows will become even more niche-oriented, and eventually will available on demand only subject to viewers' needs.

In case you think that this innovation is all driven by information technologies and internet, there are also examples of innovative new products that provide personalization without using the internet connectivity or information systems at all. A US hiking shoemaker. Rockpot, is now marketing a line of shoes with the world's first instantly customizable sole. In three minutes, it molds to the contour of your feet, to ensure a personalized comfortable fit. This also staves off future foot problems.

Predicative Modeling

Customer Relations Management (CRM) is not about call centers and sales force automation but about building organizations that focus on the customer to enable a more personalized relationship. To satisfy the desire for personalization, many tools, techniques and processes are re-engineered, re-tuned and re-built to meet the needs of the arbiter of all profit, the customer. To get closer to the customer and understand what they want at the right time, in the right place at the right price requires a little analytical effort—and has spawned data mining. Technology plays a big role but not the whole solution. The process requires a knowledge worker with in-depth domain knowledge, plus a healthy dose of intuition. Sensible questions related to customer behavior must be asked. The business analyst uses intuitive ideas and hypotheses to test the data, formulating it into a set of questions related directly to customer or business needs. A look at what is happening and what action is required to rectify an issue or create an opportunity is key. Data is stored in multi-dimensional structures.

With today's proliferation of information technology, the amount of data to be stored and understood is increasing dramatically. The data will achieve terabyte proportions very quickly and will enable predictive modeling for content management and personalization.

Companies can refine customer segmentation into meaningful sub-segments and or even micro-segments to enable more effective relationship management. They can also build channel usage models to predict the most favored channel for current and new service or product offerings.

Bank of America uses this approach to identify valuable marketing segments to offer a wide variety of personalized products packages by tweaking fees, features and interest rates. Predictive modeling also provides personalized pricing, making rock bottom prices available to customers who wouldn't otherwise buy. It increases margins on items targeted at less price-focused shoppers.

GE Capital has integrated technologies across 30 countries and 26 companies. It launched intelligent marketing campaigns to outshine its fierce competition in acquiring new customers and strengthening bonds with existing clients, using predictive modeling technologies as part of an automated and systematic way to capture customer behavior. It targets the products that best help to deepen customer relationships. GE has equipped its marketing people with the ability to: target communications to either individuals or households, apply intelligent rules to identify the right person in each household to receive specific offers; coordinate and optimize inbound and outbound communications over multiple channels, including traditional and digital media; build predictive models and combine them with other database criteria for more accurate results than rule-based approach. They can also run analysis, predictive modeling and customer communication activity from a single environment and update models automatically for any changes to customer records, ensuring that predicted outcomes always reflect the latest information.

In the future, even mass-market broadcasts will embrace predictive modeling and reflect viewers' needs. Mass-market television commercials as we know them are on their last legs. Consumers already feel they have little free time, and technology allows them to avoid irrelevant advertising. Predictive modeling will be used to find out what type of promotional or image-building messages will be served towards any individual viewer.

Mass advertising has had its day. For example, U.K.-based Abbey National Bank plans to significantly reduce its ad spending, basing its decision on research from U.K.-based Henley Center, which shows that viewers routinely ignore commercials, and instead read or send email, or switch to shopping networks while commercials air. Another study shows that 88% of TiVo users block commercials entirely. Put succinctly, if ITV or DVR-equipped viewers don't have a strong interest in commercial content, or some other incentive to watch it, they won't.

Today, the cost of producing, owning and distributing TV shows is heavily subsidized by mass-market advertising. But what happens as more mass-marketers notice their messages aren't being received? What happens as the trend toward "blocked" advertising accelerates?

DVR, ITV, VOD: unlike televisions or radio, which are one-way broadcasts are two-way interactions. TiVo and ReplayTV "know" which programs their users watch or record, and even what they transfer to VCR tapes. Wink knows which commercials and related services a customer chooses to interact with.

As VOD takes hold, expect its providers to enjoy precise knowledge of individual viewers' actions, interests and preferences. This knowledge is gathered over time in a relatively complete context. Though always honoring individual household privacy, these technology-enabling middlemen are increasingly well positioned to direct demographic and transactional data to appropriate advertisers.

Eventually, with the permission of customers, this precision will evolve to a point where anonymous yet specific customer information is actually shared with advertisers. DVR, ITV and VOD providers become data aggregators.

What does it means to advertisers? Advertisers traditionally use broadcasting to reach groups of demographically profiled, yet still largely unknown, prospects. But as ITV and DVR take hold, relatively anonymous prospects become known quantities. These are customers of firms like Wink and TiVo. If these customers agree to be pitched to by relevant advertisers, the world now shifts from broadcast advertising to middleman-assisted one-to-one prospecting. These new technologies obliterate the economics of traditional broadcasting. As compelling as this sounds, it's still a bit of a Catch-22. Technologies like DVR and ITV afford unprecedented knowledge of individual households' interests and preferences; at the same time, viewers now have control over what they watch—and given the choice, most choose not to watch commercials.

So the question becomes: how will advertisers entice viewers to (a) share information (through middlemen) and (b) accept commercials? What are the incentives the advertiser of the future can deliver? The big two are relevance ("this is a product you definitely need") and outright subsidy ("we'll pay you to hear about it") and this can only be achieved by marrying science with the art of making entertaining, personalized TV commercials. The first, most compelling and probably most demanding value proposition for any advertising will be "relevance." Why should a consumer watch this or any other promo? The ideal response would be because it's in his or her best interest. It perfectly matches the viewer's interests. Certainly, as trusted middlemen like TiVo garner enormous amounts of highly specific information about individual households and this information is shared with advertisers, the ability to achieve relevance improves. (Meanwhile, by the same reasoning, consumer tolerance for irrelevance evaporates.)

The change is coming. These technologies shatter traditional mass-marketing models. At the same time, they make each individual ad more effective. These are favorable conditions for CRM, and migrating your business strategies to the airwaves to capitalize on these rapidly evolving interactive technologies.

Peer-to-Peer Communities

The emergence of virtual communities through the use of internet technologies, connecting people with common interest from around the world is one of the most significant innovations of the network economy. Peer-to-Peer (P2P) computing has gone mainstream as millions of people exchange MP3 music files. Napster inspired other start-ups to develop many new applications for P2P networks. There are companies using P2P technologies as a way to share things beyond information.

An eBay subsidiary even provides a P2P selling community primarily for commodity media such as CDs and video games. While marketers have long understand the power of positive word of mouth through users communities, P2P technologies are the most powerful medium for building virtual-word-of-mouth communities. Consumers build their communities around subjects of interest and they can exchange product knowledge, demos and experiences across the world in real time. Marketers must master the skills of building positive virtual product communities by direct or indirect association.

In a few short years, the number of mobile phones with a camera is expected to exceed the number of digital cameras sold. The key to this is the introduction of multimedia messaging (MMS), the service that allows mobile phone users to send photographs, music as well as text in the same way they now send the hugely popular text—only SMS messages.

A New York based start-up called Upoc offers wireless service, which keeps people in touch—anywhere, anytime. With Upoc, any mobile phone is more than a phone and any pager is more than a pager. You exchange text and voice messages with groups and individuals.

Upoc sends you up-to-the-second information on the events, places, and people you're interested in - on your mobile phone or pager. You can share mobile chats on topics that you like ranging from music or movies to sports. There are hundreds of groups with topics including celebrity news, rap sheet magazine, ravers nations, inside adult entertainment and subjects that cover every large city as well many different diverse interest groups.

Procter and Gamble understands the important of peer-to-peer communications assembled a stealth sales force of 280,000 teenagers to push products to friends and families. Aged from 13 to 19 and enlisted by an arm of Procter and Gamble called Tremor. Their job is to help P&G to deliver information about their brands in living rooms, schools and other locations that are traditionally difficult to infiltrate.

These kids deliver endorsements in school cafeterias, at sleepovers and casual gatherings, by cell phone, emails, chats and SMS. It takes P&G more than two years to build this network. The idea grew out of a profound dissatisfaction among advertisers with conventional marketing. P&G uses Tremor to make a sensitive point about Head and Shoulders that it could not have broached in mainstream advertising: that the shampoo kills the fungus that causes dandruff problems. It is a message that cannot survive in the mass market. Seeing the success of peer-to-peer tactics Sony even decided to stop promoting their Net MD in print ads and engaged the service of Tremor.

As social animals all consumers have desires to have personal connection with other people. This connection has traditionally been found in many physical communities, in school, supermarkets, community centers or gymnasiums. They could even form around products, such as the Harley Davidson, McIntosh and Porsche. These communities offer value and benefits to both members and companies. Company gains include increased propensity for customers to buy and a greater ability to understand their customers and tailor their offerings. While P2P communities are very effective, the major concern is giving up control. Marketers must dream up hundreds of ways to create great a customer experience.

Gone are the days when marketers can pour money into brand advertising that plants memorable physical images and associations in consumers' minds. These tactics overlay an experience that speaks louder that headlines and slogans. In short, P2P communications will push marketing towards the collectively experiential and adapts to both the individual and collective consumer's decision-making process. It also gives "Network Marketing" its true meaning.

A Whole New Way of Thinking About Strategic Marketing

In this model, we take a holistic and strategic view of marketing as a discipline. It is a trans-functional model that approaches strategy from the customer viewpoint. The challenge for marketers is to understand what the underlying customer desires and complex behaviors mean for marketing and how to meet those needs. Which traditional marketing concepts still work, and which ones need to be eliminated or change? We believe that marketers can no longer think just functionally or use static frameworks to formulate marketing strategies.

More than ever, every functional decision impacts every other functional decision. Every decision made today has implications in the future. This systems view reflects the structural complexity as well as the dynamic complexity of the networked business environment. The new view of strategic marketing is anchored in the following three key shifts:

- The new role of technology
- The new meaning of brand
- The new economics of organization

Figure 4-4 The New Marketing Environment

The New Role of Technology

Technology today lies at the heart of almost any customer-driven marketing strategy and helps to create "customer-driven cultures". In fact, technology actually changes the nature of physical goods and products, as they increasingly become 'information enhanced or information-enabled' through the evolving relationship between customers and products.

Technology is improving marketing and customer relationships via three processes: 'Marketing Decision Support', 'Customer Feedback Cycles' and 'Mass Customization Enabling'. Instead of 'leaning back' to watch commercials with a remote control in hand, today's customers 'lean forward' to look at the screen on the internet while clicking away. They want more control and value in everything and anything they do. They expect to interact, customize and communicate as part of a community of shared interests. They have the freedom to ignore and reject. Never in the economic history of mankind have we put so much power in the hands of the customer. This forces companies that rely on traditional advertising to seriously rethink their approach.

Marketing Decision Support: Not long ago marketers believed that customer loyalty flowed naturally out of the efficient production of great products. This formula still works in a small number of industries. However, as service became a competitive weapon companies found that by creatively bundling products and services they create a lock-in effect, encouraging repeat purchases and preventing customers from switching. Operating platforms became the device for establishing an ongoing revenue stream and a migration path to higher value products or services.

Customer Feedback Cycles: This technology has the power to identify customers and track their behavior. The data and customer knowledge helps you adapt or customize products and services according to customer preferences. Airlines, hotels and car rentals companies were the first industries to leverage this concept.

Many consumer goods companies employed various approaches to create cycles of product improvement. Allowing customers to participate in the improvement of a product or service fosters a sense of "ownership" that very often translates into loyalty. Almost all e-tailers and e-content providers understand the importance of this cycle. They have personalization features built into their web sites. Using various "agent" technologies, they develop sophisticated recommendation engines based on what customers have clicked on or bought.

Mass Customization: Although not a new concept, this is only just becoming possible with the emergence of advanced technology. A wide variety of manufacturing technologies are combined with information technology allowing customers to select among a myriad of pre-defined options that are automated within the production environment. This obviously requires flexible manufacturing systems. The level of automation is very high and so are the investment costs. This led to companies that were once bitter rivals (i.e. giants of the auto industry) consolidating to finance the development costs and share the benefits. This enables them to produce and deliver personalized products at near the same costs previously achieved under mass production.

The New Meaning of Brand

Converging trends in digital infrastructure and personalization have fully transformed the brand from an image into an experience. Although this phenomenon emerged within the discipline of the retail environment, the internet is by its very nature experiential. Experiential branding requires skills and methodologies that are beyond the scope of those employed by traditional advertising agencies.

In classical brand building, the power to generate awareness and loyalty lies almost completely within your hands and those of your agency. With the customer in increasing control, you must manage interactions at all customer touch-points, from product design to purchase to delivery. The only way to manage this expanded circle of contact is to dynamically respond to the customer's view at every point of exchange, while maintaining consistency across all networks. The network economy is giving birth to the Network Brand.

To be effective, brand-building activities are integrated into a company's overall business strategy. The network brand has had an impact on activities ranging from the development of new products to the design of customer service operations to the creation of a Web site.

Overseeing how a brand affects—and is affected by—nearly every aspect of a firm's business clearly extends beyond the job description of the typical vice president of marketing. The Network Brand urgently requires the attention of the most senior managers, including the CEO.

Managers today need to understand that building brands requires the orchestration of all business processes, both internal and external, to create a network of interdependent experiences. The successful network brand is predicated on the development of sophisticated marketing tools that inform managers as to where and how brands shift customer demand.

Unlike television, which only yields ratings and print, which only yields circulation numbers, the internet tracks, measures and analyzes every user interaction in real time. The pressure to respond to an expanding network of simultaneous brand experiences, in real time, necessitates the acquisition of highly automated data literacy and behavioral analysis skills. The segmentation tools and research cycles of classical marketing are rendered woefully obsolete in this scenario.

The New Economics of the Marketing Organization

From an organizational perspective, external disaggregation appears to cause the dissolution of the marketing organization. In fact, markets are as much an organizational form as firms themselves, and both are just means of coordinating and motivating activity. They differ only in emphasis. Information liquidity causes the traditional marketing organization to shift and expand its boundaries. The internet causes marketing organizations to shift away from the "enforced cooperation" of the value chain toward the fluid dynamics of the "value network." Many firms will combine both business models, using hierarchies where tight control is needed and disaggregation where activities are outsourced. The key question now is who owns the brand, the channel and the customers as well as their data?

Summary

In predicting the future of strategic marketing, and of business as a whole, one thing is absolutely certain: the weapon of choice is an innovative response to customer behavior. Strategic marketing management using the new 4Ps together with the traditional 4Ps requires vision and creativity as well as leadership and discipline. To operate successfully in the networked environment, marketers need to extend marketing knowledge throughout the entire organization and use information liquidity as a differentiator.

Technology continues to shape interactions between marketers and customers. The battle for control of customer information between intermediaries and brand owners intensifies. The boundaries between markets and marketing organizations dissolve. The death of transactions will be followed by the rise of high-tech, high style and high-touch relationships.

You must overcome enormous barriers as you reorganize your marketing activities. The toughest challenge may not just be better understanding of the marketing implications using the "8Ps", but instilling a new marketing culture. Making the transition from a relatively simple organization structure to one in which a tightly knit marketing team with deep knowledge of the customer is dispersed throughout their organization from information technology department to operations and customer services, allows you to deliver value to consumers. It will, however, test the beliefs of even the best marketing companies.

CHAPTER 5

Pricing for Profits

It is today's business reality that every brand and even product needs to achieve a meaningful level of differentiation. Unless a firm is able to achieve a high level of differentiation through design, technology, service delivery or any combination of these, its own profits are subject to control by other competitive players.

Price is still the weapon of choice for many companies in the competition for sales and market share. The reasons are understandable. History shows that price wars have racked industry after industry. From cell phone to airlines, stock brokerage to video games producers, price has been the weapon of choice. All too often, these are wars with no winners—and few survivors. Consider the reality, no other weapon in a marketer's arsenal can be deployed as quickly, or with such certain effect.

Price discount advantages are often short-lived, and rarely balances against the long-term consequences. The worst scenario is being in a market, which consists of a "dumb" competitor and sometimes that's all it takes to start a price war. It happened in cellular phones market, and with newspapers, personal computers, film, airlines, cereal and, tobacco products. Price cut is a common way to gain market share points and managers measure marketing success from a market share perspective but not profit share. Playing the price card often is a competitive reaction and assumes significant potential gain for the firm. Usually, that's not the case. Firms start price wars when they have little to lose and much to gain; those who react to the initiators often have little to gain and much to lose.

The anticipated gains often disappear as multiple competitors join the battle and negate the lift from the initial reductions. Managers in highly competitive markets often view price cuts as the only possible strategy. They may be right sometimes, the problem is that they are playing with a very dangerous weapon in a war to improve near-term profitability. Long-term devastation may be the result.

Just as the Chinese warrior, Sun Tzu, put it, "Those who are not thoroughly aware of the disadvantages in the use of arms cannot be thoroughly aware of the advantages." If you are going to use low prices as a competitive weapon, you must be equally aware of all the risks as well as benefits. You must also learn to adjust your strategy to deploy alternatives when pricing alone is no longer effective. Failure to do so has put companies and entire industries into tailspins from which they never fully recover. Sometimes it even causes companies to go bankrupt. Kmart's long-term efforts to lower prices on thousands of items in order to compete more effectively with Wal-Mart are among the reasons cited for the company's spiral into bankruptcy.

Marketers traditionally have employed three pricing strategies: skim, penetration, and neutral. "Skim Pricing" is the process of pricing a product high relative to competitors and the product's value. "Neutral Pricing" is an attempt to eliminate price as a decision factor for customers by pricing neither high nor low relative to competitors. "Penetration Pricing" is the decision to price low relative to the product's value and to the prices of similar competitors.

Experience curve effect has always been considered as competitive weapon in hopes of driving the company to a position of market dominance. All three strategies consider how the product is priced relative to its value for customers and that of similar competitors.

When Lexus and Acura entered the luxury segment of the automobile industry, their cars' prices were high relative to standard vehicles but low relative to Mercedes and BMW. The penetration strategy was defined not by the price, but by the price relative to the value of the vehicle and to similar competitive products. Any of these strategies are associated with a variety of cost structures, and result in either profits or losses. To understand when each strategy is likely to be successful, you must evaluate your current and potential cost structure, their customers' relative price sensitivities, and your current and potential competitors. All three areas must be carefully considered before employing any pricing strategy.

Normally the price of a product or service is based upon the perceived quality and amount of its ingredients, technological advancement, level of services provided, unique product features and its brand strengths. The better these are, the higher the price you can charge. But the reverse is also true. The higher the price the higher the perceived quality. For that reason alone, companies marketing very high quality products often charge all the market can bear and promote product trials by offering promotional discounts instead of lowering prices. This works for many companies. But once a competitor decides to use pricing as strategy to gain market share, the picture changes completely. Recent examples include the PC hardware, semiconductor and cellular phone business.

A very important consideration in pricing new products, or in changing existing ones is how you expect competitors to react.

Nintendo upped the ante in the hotly contested video games market by cutting the price of its GameCube consoles by up to 24% in Europe just two weeks before its official launch. Its move followed Microsoft's decision a week before to cut the price of its Xbox consoles in Europe, putting it in line with best-selling rival, Sony's PlayStation 2 .The GameCube now retails at 100 euros cheaper than Xbox and PlayStation 2 in Europe, although the latter two come with a built-in DVD drive. Nintendo, Microsoft and Sony are battling for dominance in a $20 billion-plus (but still growing) market that now rivals the film and music industry as the favorite pastime of teens and twenty-somethings.

Video game console makers traditionally institute a price cut within the first 12 months of launch to re-ignite demand but there was industry surprise at the rapidity of the GameCube cut. Now Nintendo has imposed the cut to put further pressure on Microsoft's Xbox, which has already registered disappointing sales in markets such as Germany and France. Obviously, this was an attempt by Nintendo to put pressure on Microsoft and try to squeeze them out of the market.

Another recent example is from the telecom industry. Faced with huge network-spending bills, a looming slowdown in subscriber growth and tightened capital markets, the last thing the industry needs is a price war to ravage balance sheets even more. But the "price pressure" crackle is heard through the wireless world everyday. Customers in most major U.S. markets have six players to choose from. Meanwhile, the pool of virgin mobile-phone users is constantly shrinking, currently sitting at a little more than 35% of the U.S. population.

Naturally, vendors will have to try harder to get their desired share at a time when leading enroller Sprint PCS is signing up more than 1 million customers a month. Accordingly, phone makers prepare for more than 50% of the worldwide shipments of handsets in 2005 to be sold as replacement phones. A high-growth market can only sustain exponential increases for so long, and in the U.S., investors spent months moping over the realization that the American wireless-industry hockey stick flattened.

The U.S. is unique in its wireless free-for-all. In Europe, growth has slowed as penetration reaches similar rates, but carriers on the continent typically benefit from having only one or two main competitors in each market. While the Federal Communications Commission may have benefited wireless consumers by avoiding the monopoly situations that dominate in the cable and local-telephone markets, wireless carriers face a competitive scenario similar to the long-distance phone business. Like that realm, wireless has given consumers a dizzying array of choices from bundled calling plans to features. All that's missing from the long-distance comparison are the fallout and the many failures. Carriers are gearing their market toward expanded calling plans, while making less money on call minutes spent on the phone.

The incentive to call more was basically the wrong behavior. It necessitates more capital spending. Heavy calling doesn't pay for itself. Instead, carriers must try to differentiate their offerings with something other than price, be it a more reliable network or a killer feature offering. Marketing needs to go beyond price to win out in this game.

So what can a company do in these situations and what are the consequences associated with of each of these options? Companies with strong existing brands and wide product ranges could try one of the following strategies:

-   Hold prices the same
-   Lower prices on selective models only
-   Lower prices to the same level of the new brand
-   Lower prices of leading brand even further
-   Use promotional bundles or manufacturers' rebates
    to compensate for price differences

Such situations confront marketers all the time. If you understand the tools and concepts used to manage competitive pricing as part of marketing tactics, your firm will have an edge in the marketplace. Understanding likely competitive response is as critical as understanding customer needs. This chapter addresses the role of pricing in determining your marketing positioning; the importance of price tiers in a marketplace and how price is used to manage competitors effectively and push for profitability.

Price, more than most product attributes, effectively defines your competitive position. It is, as we have discussed, a major factor in how your product is perceived vis a vis the competition. Brands or products are aligned on a "value map" of perceived product value versus price to effect tiers. Three or four tier markets are common (i.e. best, premium, good and value). Any firm may have products covering one or more of these tiers.

The appropriate number of tiers in any market is situation-specific. Sometimes markets are viewed as two-tier, namely "branded" and "non-branded". Some markets can have as many as seven or eight tiers. Automobile and personal financial services products typically have the largest number of tiers. Very early in the development or planning process, positioning implies a strategy, a relevant competitive set and a price range. Target pricing decisions are made very early in the development process by carefully considering the strategic marketing implications.

It is also common for companies to reverse the process and market a product at a specific price range with a certain set of features. In short, price determines cost—not the other way round. Companies like Compaq, IBM, Sony and Apple have all used this strategy. In order to calculate and control the ultimate go-to-market price, sometimes they might compromise on quality, features or launch time. Apple waited for almost 8 months to launch their new flat-screen iMac because they wanted to wait till the prices of LCD screens fell to the $300 price range. This allowed them to be able to offer the product at $1,500.00. Extensive cross-industry research indicates that:

- All competition within a price-tier is usually more vigorous than across tiers.
- There is an asymmetry in competition across tiers. Price cuts are more effective when offering products from a higher tier than when a lower tier firm tries to pull customer from upper tiers through price cuts.

- The macro economic environment has different impacts on various tiers. Some top tier products are less affected by a recession than middle tier products. Lowest tier products are also less impacted by a recession.

Past research has shown that price leadership is a strategy that is usually open to a large firm in an industry. These are companies with strong brands, channel or other market power to set a price that most other firms follow.

From the outset companies decide whether they have the market might to be the price leader or whether they must accept the realty that they have to be price followers. The latter are usually smaller firms; less known brand names but sometimes market leaders that dominate their particular markets. Sometimes they enjoy a good profit margin and a certain degree of brand. They may not need to use pricing as a competitive weapon as the price set by the leader is sufficient for them to maintain a good bottom line.

A capacity limit (such as that faced by airlines, hotel chains) necessitates a specific load factor to enjoy good margins. Once the load factor is controlled, pricing strategies are more flexible.

Products that indicate quality by price (usually products whose value is difficult to quantify) such as cosmetic and personal care products also have flexibility in pricing strategy.

In a research study 28 brands in four frequently purchased package goods categories were analyzed. Results showed that competitors in the same tier are typically most negatively impacted by a price cut. These are consequently the companies most likely to react when one of its competitors institutes such a cut.

One research analyzed twenty-eight brands in four frequently purchased consumer packaged-goods categories and discovered that higher priced, higher quality brands steal share from other brands in the same quality tier and brands in the tier below. However, lower-price, lower quality brands take share from their own tier and the tier-below brands, but do not steal significant shares from higher tiers.

Higher quality brands usually have a significant advantage in their ability to induce consumers to enter the market through a price cut or promotional sale. One study indicates that a 10% cut in the price of a high quality consumer packaged goods item induces a 5 to 6% share point rise due to new customers entering the market. Lower tier products do not have this power and they usually gain less than 1% in share points.

Figure 5-1 Cross Channels Price Sensitivities

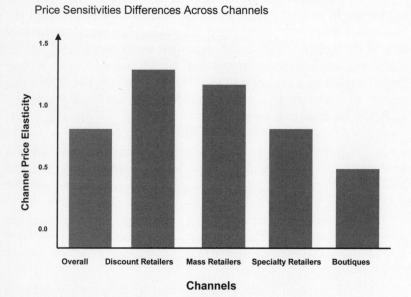

Price Sensitivities Differences Across Channels

As you consider the notion of price tiers, determine how many of those tiers your products cover and focus on same tier competition. You should also analyze each competitor's drawing power.

Most market leaders and their brands are very powerful, but sometimes limited to existing customers. I refer to this as passive power. Innovative products and technologies can sometimes develop active power in a short period of time and attract new customers.

Effective price management requires a deep understanding of these two fundamentally different types of power.

The biggest headache for many marketers is when the market appears to be competing purely on price and price alone. The only way to deal with this is to develop a better understanding of competitors and their behaviors. This allows you to anticipate their pricing moves and reactions and determine how to influence and shape yours.

Penetration pricing is getting more and today, even for new innovative products where marketers usually prefer a skimming strategy. This helps recover R&D costs and exploits some first mover advantages. The hyper-competitive environment, however, often leads to penetration pricing strategy that has the following advantages:

- It enables marketers to cover a mass market in a shorter period of time before competition can respond.
- It creates a customer lock-in effect, particularly for products that requires consumer learning.
- It deters potential new entrants by pricing below the normal target amount of return.
- It helps improve demand, which means the company can move down the learning curve.
- It moves products that have a highly elastic demand where the high price segment is too small to support the business.

Empirical research shows that there is a high degree of pricing interdependence among competing firms. Consequently pricing is highly influenced by the pricing of others. A study by Lambin shows an elasticity of 0.71, which means that on average, a 10% decrease was met by a 7.1% decrease in competitor's pricing. Competitive response varies greatly by situation. Here are some examples:

- Kodak once held more than 70% of the $2 billion US film market and still holds significant share. If competitor, Fuji, cut its price, would Kodak follow?

- IBM today still holds significant share in personal computers, particularly in the corporate market. If Dell decides to cut its prices across its product lines, does IBM follow?
- USAir, a key player in domestic short haul flights, decides to cut its price on the New York-Boston shuttle route. Does Delta follow?
- Microsoft holds more than 90% market share in the personal PC operating system market. If Linux is offering a compatible OS for a fraction of the cost of Windows XP or even free of charge, does Microsoft follow?

Obviously in the first instance, Kodak, with high brand equity and market share, would certainly respond to Fuji's price cut. Just a 5% cut would cost Kodak at least $50 million in revenues. Yet Fuji has the luxury of a big domestic market to support a price war with both revenue and scale-based advantage perspectives. Is it the same for IBM and Dell? Dell, the most efficient PC manufacturer with a direct-to-customer model, is in an excellent position to use price cuts to drive out players or drive market share up. In the case of Microsoft, the market leader both in OS and general office applications would have little to worry about even if Linux offers a free OS. Firms often try to be the first one to undercut others to gain market share.

Using economic theory to see this problem, the Bertrand outcome is a Nash equilibrium in this case but it is not necessary subgame perfect. The interpretation of the subgame perfect equilibrium is that firms behave nicely towards each other, unless it pays to fight.

To illustrate this in a duopoly context, it only pays a firm to fight its competitors if they are substantially weaker or less efficient than the firm. If all firms have similar cost structures, it is more profitable to be "nice", and not start price wars.

Figure 5-2 Drivers of Industry Price Behavior

Ten Factors that Drive Industry Price Behavior

Industry Characteristics	Price War	
	Low Risk	High Risk
Product Characteristics	Highly Differentiated	Highly Commoditized
Service Characteristics	Highly Personalized	Highly Standardized
Technological Advancement	Rapid Pace	Slow Pace
Capacity Utilization	High	Low
Customer Concentration	Widely Dispersed	Highly Concentrated
Price Visibility	Low	High
Barriers to Switch	High	Low
Customer Price Sensitivity	Low	High
Intensity of Competition	Low	High
Medium Term Cost Trend	Stable	Declining

A rise in the number of firms in any market place or an increase in efficiency or scale-economics for any one firm raises the equilibrium price by reducing the incentive to behave aggressively. The main idea is the cost distribution in an industry is a major determinant of how competitive or aggressive firm are. The cost gaps between firms are the main driving factor. An analysis of price wars in several industries also reveals certain factors that determine a competitor's strategic intent and most likely response. These factors include:

- Overall cost structure: Industries such as cellular services, airlines and newspapers have a very high fixed cost but low variable cost structure. They can offer the next customer the same product or service at close to zero variable cost. Hence, almost any incremental revenue a new customer brings makes it worth pursuing. This is true also with technology-based services since there is almost no decreasing return impact.

- Total capacity utilization: There is tremendous overcapacity today in many industries from telcos to semiconductors. Hence, there is an excellent opportunity for each player to take on customers with their variable cost being the only cost impact.
- Flexibility of capacity adjustment: If capacity is not effectively adjusted downward because of exit barriers, low capacity utilization persists and encourages price competition.
- Capacity in many today industries is easily ramped up at very little cost, in particularly for software-driven business models.
- The degree to which a product is perishable. Hotel rooms, cruises and airline seats cannot be inventoried for sale another day. So there is a motivation in moving these perishable goods at whatever incremental revenues they bring in.
- The extent of product/service differentiation: The level of industry differentiation that exists is key as it allows customers to use substitutes. Lack of differentiation in the form of service, design and technology can trigger a price war more easily.
- Structure diversity of competition: If all competitors have the same cost of capital, buy from the same source, and use the same manufacturing process, method and operate under similar business models, everyone has very similar cost structures.
- Efficiency of buying: The degree in which customer can find out about competitive prices and the effort required to do so. Some industries make it very difficult to directly compare prices due to complexity of pricing structure.
- Brand Loyalty: To what extent customers are locked by way of liking the brand and its products or specific relationships that are built over an extended period of time.
- Overall industry growth rate: If the industry pie is not growing or the growth is slow, players are tempted to expand aggressively to grow market share by price war.
- Impact of complementary products: Price competition increases if a purchase of the product has a secondary revenue impact. Examples include computer games consoles. Once a customer buys a certain console from Sony or

Nintendo, he buys all their software. Price cuts help build and expand an installed base.

In many cases, industry profitability depends on the collective wisdom of the players. It takes only one "dumb" player to start a sometimes irreversible price war. This occurred in the airlines and cellular phone industry.

You must consider industry wide profitability using price as a market-share building tool. Marketers must change their "market share" mind set changes to a "profit share" mind set.

When many internet firms needed to boost their customer base they turned to price cutting and ultimately offering their services for free. The next new entrant entered the market by going one step further—giving away money to customers. Their logic was the same —forgoing short-term profitability to build long term positioning through market share. This aggressive pursuit of market share led to over-capacity, aggressive price-cutting and zero profitability industries.

What really matters are not share of market, share of voice, share of stomach or share of mind, it's the share of profits or "market surplus". The smart stance is to take a wider view of the market beyond your own organization to see the whole industry's market surplus and encourage competition to do the same. Failure to do so has caused profits to be elusive in many industries from long distance carriers to cable service and internet service providers.

Sometimes downward adjustment is necessary both at a firm level or industry level. Such a move must be accomplished in so that it does not spiral out of control. It is a common practice to push for an industry shakeout and adjustment in capacity. What usually happens is the shakeout extends beyond the target and time anticipated and adjustment is over-estimated.

Three things need to be considered: the action, the competitor perception of the action and the competitors' counter-action. A few important questions to ask yourself when planning for such action are:

- How would I like my competitors to respond to my price cut or other complimentary offerings relating to the offer?
- Would this offer likely grow the overall market or simply take share from my competitors?
- Who and to what extent will our competitors follow?
- How likely is it that my most direct competitor's response will not be cutting price but finding ways to stress differentiation?

Here are a few common mistakes to avoid:

- Pricing should always take the channel considerations into account and include ways to provide operation.
- When focusing on customer value don't divorce pricing from the rest of the marketing mix. Product, communications and distribution all go hand in hand with pricing.
- Consider customizing pricing since failing to understand the value equation requirements of different segments often loses profit opportunities.
- Uniformity in gross margin for channel partners is common and typically stems from a cost-driven principle or failure to understand the customer value equation. Deep understanding of customer value requirements at the appropriately disaggregate level allows more precise and profitable matching of price value.
- Pricing also needs to reflect product life cycle considerations.

Here are a number of ways to determine pricing other than subjective judgment:

- **Historical Data Analysis**: With good company sales and product data as well as competitive prices, you can estimate a demand curve. If price changes are in the range of prices in the data and if competitive response does not change, the estimated elasticity can be used as benchmark.

- **Customer Survey**: Purchase intention studies are inexpensive with specific products at specific prices. Using different prices with different random examples then generate a demand curve. Sometimes larger samples are required if you wish to describe the product and ask willingness to pay a single price and rotate that price across random examples.
- **Economic Value to Customer**: If a product replaces another that is currently being used, then EVC analysis can be used to demonstrate the additional benefits. These benefits can then being translated into dollars. The net benefits are the difference between the benefits and the additional costs— added to the reference price is the value of your product. Usually returns some surplus benefit to the consumer and charges a price lower than the value. This needs to combine EVC analysis in combination with some beta testing.
- **Conjoint Analysis**: This is often used to measure tradeoffs customers make in terms of features and prices. When the price is one of the attributes in the conjoint design, the attributes are rescaled to reflect how much the customer is willing to pay for any specific attribute.

Another challenge area is the pricing of bundled products or services. The concept of product bundling is not new and is extremely common, particularly among software or service businesses that are incorporated into product packages and sold at a bundled price.

The individual components of the bundle may or may not be available on a standalone basis. If they are also sold separately, then the bundled price is generally lower that the sum of items purchased individually.

There are numerous examples of bundling, from cellular phone bundled with short messaging service packages, digital cameras bundled with photo manipulation software programs, cable TV digital decoders bundled with movie on demand packages, video game consoles bundled with games, personal computers bundled with inkjet printers and software packages, credit cards bundled with insurance products as well as stock brokerage accounts bundled with private banking services.

Bundling creates leverage by increasing returns on product changes and raising the barriers to market entry, thereby increasing freedom pricing flexibility.

In the early stage of new product introduction, bundling speeds innovation diffusion by reducing customers' uncertainties. Later in the product lifecycle, bundling is effective for those who want to pursue differentiation. Bundled pricing is regarded as a very effective tactical tool.

How the bundle is priced directly determines how a company benefits from the strategy. Improperly executed, bundling fails to generate the level of sales anticipated, or it may cannibalize other successful product lines. Bundled pricing is managed dynamically. As the market evolves, marketers must continually review and, when necessary, adjust the price of the bundle. How should we price the bundle so as to fully benefit from this strategy? There are a number of situations we first need to consider:

- When buyers have little information about the price. Pricing the bundled offering is no different from pricing other, unbundled new products. The only considerations are the overall positioning of the product in the marketplace and how the perceived value of the bundle and the brand strength compares with the proposed price. This approach to pricing the bundle works as long as the manufacturer can suppress or virtually control prices of the various components. However, when, customers learn the prices of some of the items (and they will) pricing becomes a very different issue.
- When buyers know how much some or all of the components costs for the bundled offering is attractive if it is 1/ cheaper than purchasing the individual components separately or 2/ more convenient or reliable, or 3/ all of the above.
- The requirement that the price of the bundle is lower than the total price of its components, plus search, aggregation and transaction costs, offers insight into why bundling is most effective early in the life cycle of an innovation. Consequently, finding alternative sources of the components, obtaining the necessary components, assembling them and

104

recreating the bundle is both expensive and risky. By comparison the bundled offering is attractive.

- For bundling to be successful, marketers must either lower the costs of producing the bundle to a level required for customer acceptance; control or raise prices of components sold separately or concentrate on the more risk-averse segments of the market or those segments where the perceived opportunity costs are high and the return is high. It is not uncommon for banks, equipment or utility providers to make their service bundle more attractive by raising their prices for additional services or non-contract service calls and parts through extended warranty programs.

Another tough challenge in crafting smart pricing strategies is dealing with the cross-channel environment.

For example if an airline or hotel offers its seats or rooms at different prices through online direct booking, online travel agents and online discount agents, at the same time, a customer learns of the price difference between channels. Since products are almost identical the most expensive channels tend to suffer loss of market share. The internet is a great price equalizer since it provides price transparency. Pricing issues that arise as a result of price transparency almost always create conflict and undermine standard channels. There are two ways to deal with this problem.

One way is to limit your customers' ability to play arbitrage games (purchasing identical products or services, or combinations of both, through more than one channel.) In other words, the supplier's value proposition comprises much more than simple unit product or service pricing. This is easier said than done in the case of airlines and hotel, since the only tools that are available are cancellations policies, and flexibility in making changes.

Companies must find new ways to create service bundles to differentiate their value propositions. Look for opportunities to target segments whose wants and needs have yet been addressed properly. The internet is an excellent way to allow customers to create personalized products or services that might otherwise be uneconomical through physical channels or when a high level of privacy is desired.

There is no single best way to create a pricing strategy. I hope this chapter provides some useful guidelines. The cost-plus pricing approach is simple. It is also the most commonly used due to the fact all costs needed to be covered in the long run. However such matters are never that simple, since in multi-product and service inclusive situations certain fixed costs are allocated. Those allocations are not precise and numbers usually just come out of the blue.

A slightly better way of pricing uses a combination of all three: cost-plus, competitor and customer value based pricing. The logic here is that competitive prices reveal shared wisdom about industry collective response. Customer-value based pricing reflects your differentiation and this requires a deep understanding of your customers and their purchase behavior. Remember, theory and research will only get you halfway; the "art" of pricing is learned in the battlefield.

CHAPTER 6

Marketing Innovative Products

What is an innovative product or service? Over the years researchers have come up with three basic different frameworks to distinguish truly innovative products from next-step improvements of existing ideas: technical vs. market-related, evolutionary vs. revolutionary, and sustaining vs. disruptive.

Technological innovations involve creating knowledge of components, linkages between components, methods, processes, and techniques that go into a product or service.

Business or market innovations involve knowledge of distribution channels, product applications, and consumer expectations, preferences, needs, and wants. The product or service is new in that its cost is lower, its attributes are improved, it has attributes it never had before, or it never existed in that market before". The first microprocessor was a technological innovation, because it came from knowledge that had never existed before. Dell's business model is a business innovation, because it came from knowledge of a combination of distribution channels and inventory management that never existed before.

An evolutionary product is one that is an extension of an existing technology and is typically compatible with older, established technologies but incompatible with new, competitive technologies.

In contrast, a revolutionary technology is one that does not offer compatibility with existing technologies but may offer superior performance.

Figure 6-1 Examples of Innovative Products That Are Not Compatible

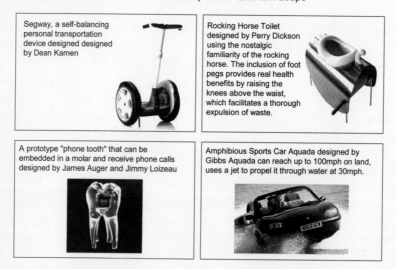

Examples of Innovative Products that Represent Quantum Leaps

Segway, a self-balancing personal transportation device designed designed by Dean Kamen

Rocking Horse Toilet designed by Perry Dickson using the nostalgic familiarity of the rocking horse. The inclusion of foot pegs provides real health benefits by raising the knees above the waist, which facilitates a thorough expulsion of waste.

A prototype "phone tooth" that can be embedded in a molar and receive phone calls designed by James Auger and Jimmy Loizeau

Amphibious Sports Car Aquada designed by Gibbs Aquada can reach up to 100mph on land, uses a jet to propel it through water at 30mph.

Each new Intel Pentium microprocessor is an evolutionary technology because it is compatible with pre-existing computer hardware and software. However, the standards war between VHS and Betamax, Windows and Mac OS, SACD and DVDA, DVD-R and DVD-Ram, DVD and DVHS all represent revolutionary technologies that are incompatible with existing technologies and with one another.

The biggest battle in the consumer product standard arena will probably be the battle of the TV operating system. The world's top electronic makers are working together and rallying around an operating system other than Windows. It is a battle to turn TVs into idiot-proof replacements for PCs.

While it is getting harder and harder to tell the difference between the hardware in the living room and the PC in the study, home devices that store, play and edit music and videos are beginning to resemble a PC and vice versa. A rift in the software to run the multi-media home is now open and will guarantee a tough battle even for an industry giant like Microsoft. All electronics giants—including Samsung, Sony, Philips, and Panasonic—have united behind using Linux and plan to phase out their own proprietary systems. Over time, all sorts of consumer electronics will connect to one another and the internet using Linux—an open system that reveal its code to anyone.

Sustaining versus Disruptive

Sustaining technologies improve the performance of established products, along the dimensions of performance that mainstream customers in major markets have historically valued.

In contrast, disruptive technologies "result in worse performance, at least in the near term. Disruptive technologies under-perform established products in mainstream markets. They have, however, certain unique features that a particular segment of customers or markets finds valuable. Products based on disruptive technologies are typically either cheaper, simpler, smaller, easier to use or sometimes perform tasks in the background without the user knowing it.

Each successive generation of 3Com's popular Palm personal digital assistant (the Palm IIIx, the Palm V) has been a sustaining technology, because it represents an incremental improvement over previous versions. Usually the level of backward compatibility is the most difficult consideration since this can be a key factor in determining whether this is a sustaining or disruptive new product. But the original Apple Newton (and its progeny) as well as IBM and Microsoft pen-based computers are all intended to be disruptive technologies, because they represent a radical alternative to paper organizers but performed more poorly than the status quo.

Technical versus Market-related

The technical versus market-related framework developed by Alan Afuah is a workhorse definition that is useful for dividing the realm of innovation into two camps.

An example of a technical innovation is the original Macintosh computer that introduced new concepts and features, such as the GUI interface, into the market.

Conversely, the iMac is a market-related innovation since it bundles existing technology in an inventive way, satisfying consumer demand for an "internet" computer.

Another example is Sony's first Walkman. It was not a technical innovation but merely married a small tape player and a set of headphones, thereby creating a new product or even a new product category.

However, a portable MP3 digital player such as Apple iPod is a technical innovation and requires solving many technical issues.

While Afuah's framework is useful, it does not provide a scale for measuring the relative degree of innovation between two products in a certain arena. One interesting way to look at it is to assess whether the voice of technology vs. the voice of the customers contributes more to its development.

Evolutionary versus Revolutionary

Carl Shapiro and Hal Varian characterize innovations as either evolutionary or revolutionary. They define an evolutionary product as the next generation version of that product, such as the Pentium III.

In contrast, a revolutionary product does not follow the sales and acceptance path and may not be compatible with previous versions of the product.

For example, in the 90's Corning felt that color TV was a revolutionary product that required sales forecasting models similar to the original introduction of television instead of building off demand forecasts for their latest black and white model. While this model seems useful in the abstract, it tends to break down when applied to real products and services.

For example, did liquid Tide represent an evolutionary or revolutionary step in detergents? The invention of the fast-food chain was a revolution in food service, yet it had its roots in the roadside food stalls that have existed since antiquity.

One could almost identity a revolutionary versus evolutionary technology by the way that the sales force and the developers receive it. If the product is evolutionary, offering more features on an existing product, the sales force is pleased and the developers are not. If it is revolutionary, representing a new way of solving a particular issue, the developers are happy and the sales force is disgruntled.

The main problem with the evolutionary/revolutionary framework is that it starts from a common premise or definition of a customer need and provides a way of segmenting two possible responses. Let's focus on really innovative new ideas, the innovations that create paradigm shifts, change industry market power structures, change the definitions of product-markets, customer behaviors and their needs and the best technology to meet those needs.

Figure 6-2 Innovative Product Taxonomies

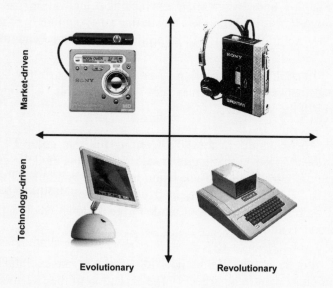

Market-driven

Technology-driven

Evolutionary   Revolutionary

Disruptive Technologies

Perhaps the most useful tool to use to analyze innovative products and technologies is Clayton Christensen's sustaining versus disruptive framework. It differs from Shapiro and Varian by creating a category —disruptive innovations—for paradigm-shifting innovations that change the entire nature of the market as well as its behavior. While revolutionary products such as the VCR or the color television are often very profitable for their inventors, disruptive innovations often are not. Their true impacts often not recognized until an extended period of time has passed.

A disruptive technology challenges many previously held assumptions and threatens all the painfully acquired knowledge bases —not only internally (within a company) but also externally with customers that use it. The introduction of a disruptive technology is an incredibly painful process. Like a hurricane or a tornado, it wipes out or makes obsolescent the years spent learning languages and systems, investing in tools and programs, acquiring market knowledge and information.

The makers of buggy whips, slide rules, super-sized mainframes, are going to fight disruptive technology tooth and nail. Their established customers, heavily invested in the old technology, generally do not welcome it with open arms either. Adding insult to injury, disruptive technologies are often dismal failures in their first effort. Sales of the original Mac were dismal. Apple's failure with the Newton, an early model of PDA is legendary. IBM discontinued its TransNote, a pen-based series of computers to address how people record information within months of launching it and Iridium failed miserably with its global satellite phone even with strong backing from parent company Motorola.

So why should you bother with disruptive technologies? The short answer is: they cannot be stopped. If we stop pressing the exterior boundaries of knowledge, progress ceases and we'd still be living in a Newtonian world (or an Aristotelian one). R&D departments in companies are continually coming up with potentially disruptive new ideas. They will never be short of them. The trick is how to manage and create value from them.

Second, disruptive technologies are profitable, sometimes incredibly profitable, if you can take advantage of them. Look at the engineers who left Fairchild to found Intel, or Oracle's success with IBM's relational database. Disruptive technologies create whole new categories of products and services and are perhaps the underlying drivers of the economy.

Andy Grove of Intel describes disruptive technologies as "10x changes": When a change in how some element of one's business is conducted becomes an order of magnitude larger than what that business is accustomed to, then all bets are off. There's wind and then there's a typhoon, there are waves and then there's a tsunami. There are competitive forces and then there are super competitive forces.

Finally, ignoring disruptive technologies is an excellent prescription for going out of business. As, John Seely Brown of PARC explained, "Innovations are going to come that will threaten our revenue streams. We want to be the ones controlling those innovations".

Therefore, companies need a process for creating and managing disruptive technologies. Intelligent companies avoid some of the "pain" of disruptive technologies by structuring their organizations and marketing efforts to take advantage of the benefits and reduce the risks that such technologies offer. In the following two sections, we will outline steps you can take to build better organizations and conduct better market research to turn those disruptive technologies into home runs.

So what causes innovative products and technologies to fail?

Innovative product launches are "binary events". They are worthless or highly lucrative and usually nothing in between. High risks and high return.

So what causes some products to succeed while other fail miserably? Many products don't even get a chance to go market. Products sometimes fail because they cannot deliver the promised capability, or attract enough interest. Even if you can demonstrate potential, it might take a lot longer that expected to reach the projected market.

It took more than 20 years to convince the public it needed zippers. Even then, they were not adopted because of "needs", "product benefits" or that button flies did not work, but because of cultural ideas about modernity and fashion trend. Personal cellular phones were around for a long time and their growth in the US was stagnant. It took a horrifically tragic event in New York for people to realize the security benefits of cell phones.

When things go very wrong it is usually due to one or more than one of the following reasons:

- The new technologies behind the products is not linked to an exciting and worthwhile market opportunity.
- The technology applications do not fully demonstrate its market potential.
- Adequate knowledge and resources for marketing that drives consumer adoption are lacking.
- The market constituents for gaining market acceptance are not mobilized.
- The products are not shown or understood in context.
- The consumer adoption rate and curve is miscalculated.
- Products are not positioned within any product category.
- The products are pushed to an often skeptical customer group without neutralizing perceived risks associated with the new products.
- The application is limited to a small niche market and is not appropriate for mass-market needs due to its nature of price.

The key to successful marketing of technologies is to seeing commercialization as a process of "value recognition". It starts very early in the development stage. There's always innovation, but the innovators do not necessarily create value. Innovation in and of itself merely creates "potential value" if it meets a need.

Marketing's role is to recognize that value by matching the innovation to the customers whose needs it can meet. Before the product is fully developed, marketing efforts should commence. In the history of videocassette recorder, RCA and Ampex, pioneers in the early video recording business, both gave up long before a mass-market product had been developed. Panasonic and Sony, by contrast, benefiting from the "free-rider" benefits went on to make thousands of improvements in design and engineering. The initial concept for RCA and Ampex was to target professional editing for recording studios and TV stations. Sony and Panasonic realized that there might be a mass domestic market for the product if its performance could be enhanced. The VCR was then transformed into one of Japan's largest export products. Many people still believe that being the first with an innovative product or technology has a much better chance of success. History shows us that is not necessarily so. We need to consider winning not only in the short term but also in the long run.

The story of the 35mm camera is a perfect example. In the early twentieth century, many inventors played with the idea of still photo cameras using the 35mm format. It was a very radical idea at that time as a huge box camera with large negative plates was the standard.

In 1914, Oscar Barnack, then an optical engineer at Ernst Leitz Optische Werke, a leading German manufacturer of microscopes and telescopes, built a hand-made crude 35mm camera although the company did not consider themselves to be in the camera business. Ultimately Ernst Leitz agreed to invest in what might be an emerging market for a killer product, which was the first "hand-held" camera.

The first introduction was a stunning success with 1,600 cameras sold. They enjoyed sustained success due to lens quality and precision. Leica became the "Mercedes" of cameras. The success spawned copycats in the years that followed, particularly from Japan.

The first Japanese competitor came from Kwanon. They later changed their name to Canon. Then Nikon, a third firm engaged a team of German optical engineers. Nikon introduced its first camera in 1946 and enjoyed years of success in the professional and amateur markets. In 1959 Nikon introduced the extremely successful "F" SLR camera.

Leica ignored the competition and did not introduce its "Leicaflex SLR" until 1965. By that time, Nikon occupied the position of "professional" camera status versus Leicaflex for the amateur. Leica still stood out as the symbol of technological excellence in photography. Photographs found in Life and Time magazines were almost always taken with a Leica. The combination of quality and market dominance built up a near-cult brand loyalty for Leica. So what went wrong?

Their problem was finally diagnosed many years later by a senior executive as follows: "The company is too proud of its history and forgot all about the present and the future."

They ended up paying a hefty price. Despite much that has been written about the "first mover" advantages, the lesson here is "first mover advantages" are often offset by "first mover disadvantages". These include "free-rider effects" and "copycat advantages". No matter how technologically superior a product is, marketing needs to begin very early even when the company is enjoying dominant success.

Another example that does not involve any technology is Diners Club, founded in 1950 by Francis McNamara and his lawyer Robert Schneider, originally positioned as a prestige service for traveling businessmen or salesmen.

The charge card was more than an innovative new product; it ushered in an entirely new lifestyle. Diners Club worked very hard trying to overcome two major challenges. They had to convince merchants that by accepting the card customers would spend more. They also needed to overcome consumer attitudes towards credit. They enjoyed success for a few years until American Express entered the market. The latter took advantage of "free-rider" effects since Diners Club had already educated the market about the benefits of a charge card. Armed with an extensive computer mailing list, savvy marketing know-how and a well-respected brand name, they employed and pioneered sophisticated direct marketing tools and grew market share in a short period of time.

By the end of 1959, they signed up 500,000 cardholders and the card was accepted at more than 32,000 locations. As American Express roared ahead with aggressive marketing, Diners Club was losing members at a rate of 5,000 per week. American Express blitzed the market with product extensions including a "corporate card' for business use. The company extended the brand with unsurpassed success through its "gold" and "platinum" card launches.

Another serious challenge in defining the potential of any commercialization, which is estimating the market potential as well as the time it takes to reach a reasonable percentage of its users, while the product is still in development stage. If you are not sure exactly what you are making, how do you estimate how many people will buy them and how much they will pay? This challenge of marrying a new product's function with market-worthy end products lies behind many delays and cost overruns in the commercialization process. It is extremely rare for products, no matter how well conceived and demonstrated, to be immediately well received by the marketplace. 40% made it only to the pilot test stage and 85% did not get further funding to go to market.

Visionary marketing begins at the "functional threshold", a point at which product use is demonstrated successfully and its value within the context of any particular group of users is clear. This usually requires a wide range of concepts, data, and heuristics. It must be a demonstration of application-specific utility that those judging the development find convincing. At this stage, the products usually are used in a variety of applications and markets. The scope and attractiveness of the product contribute as much to the future viability as its technical achievements.

This is where marketing begins. It is key to have access to potential market applications or any technological breakthrough will die. You must understand its various potential uses and explore all of them thoroughly and systematically. This might include conceiving the right product platforms, right vertical industries, or right categories, which are leveraged across a family of different products. Here are the general considerations to determine and choose applications:

- Step back from your company business boundaries and consciously look beyond the initial context for which the product or technology was developed;
- Try to avoid predictive bias by defining applications from a use standpoint, that is the preoccupation with current collective dominant logic so to avoid the "mega-mistakes"; and
- Construct and map out a detailed portfolio of applications that optimize return on investment over time.

Exploring Applications

The best way to do this is to deal with these considerations in a number of separate stages. Innovative ideas and technologies are not intrinsically marketable. They are made commercially viable through marketing. Your task is to:

- Take the technologies or initial products a few steps further and explore the best possible applications;
- Craft an attractive strategy to pursue these applications and mobilize both internal and external resources quickly and effectively while demonstrating the applications;
- Map out patent protection, strategic alliance planning and initial market feasibility studies etc.

As very few products in this world work on a totally stand-alone basis, you must start thinking about your first marketing target. There are usually three basic sets of market constituents to contend with. These are: companies that take part in the marketing and/or delivery of the new products; advocates that play a role in its market acceptance and companies that are already commercializing the incumbent products or technologies. The first group can consists of:

- Early adopters (people who have special reasons, needs or interest in using, marketing or selling the products).
- Manufacturers or components providers who can potentially produce part or all of the final products.

- Distributors with strong market power and access to customers that play some co-marketing role.
- Other companies who produce, supply or market complementary products and/or services that bundle or enhance the new products' usage or performance.

Mobilizing and marketing to these market constituents requires a careful analysis of the entire products value chain and business system. Such influences and market power must be assessed at each stage. With new technology you must deliver beyond the existing industry structure to determine how this would fit in with other forces that are shaping the industry. Once identified, the next step is to align the interest of different market constituents and design a way to share the potential benefits with them.

For radical technologies or products, market constituents will be of far greater importance. Companies who are too focused on their own product development effort often ignore this critical stage.

At this point, you should look for an early forecast to assess the potential size of the market. There is usually a lot of misunderstanding about what kind of forecasting needs to be employed. The following list includes the most commonly used and effective approaches:

Forecasting the Market of the Future – Tools and Techniques

Forecasting has long been important to marketing practitioners. A recent survey of 134 U.S. companies, found that 99% prepared forecasts when they used formal marketing plans. In another study, more than 90% of the companies sampled indicated that sales and marketing forecasting was one of the most critical functions, or a "very important" aspect of their company's success.

Forecasting needs vary considerably. Some may wish to forecast the size and growth of a market or product category. By forecasting costs and using the sales forecast, one can forecast profits and other financial outcomes. Although the usefulness of formal forecasting is sometimes questioned it is likely due to forecasts inaccuracy; unrealistic expectations about accuracy or emergence of issues when forecast results conflict with beliefs about the future.

This chapter briefly explains the rationale each approach, discusses the ways in which each forecasting approach is used, and indicates whether results are typically quantitative or qualitative in nature. The techniques are categorized by the five different ways people see the future:

- **Extrapolators**
- **Pattern Finders**
- **Market Shapers**
- **Flexible Adapters**
- **Intuition Followers**

Each of these approaches has its advantages as well as shortcomings. I find more effective forecasts usually result from the use of more than one approach.

Extrapolators

The future often represents a logical extension of the past. Large scale, inexorable forces drive the future in a continuous, reasonably predictable manner. One can; therefore, best forecast the future by identifying past trends and extrapolating them in a reasoned, logical manner.

Technology Trend Analysis is based on the observation that advances in technologies tend to follow an exponential improvement process. The technique uses early improvement data to establish the rate of progress and extrapolates that rate to project the level of progress at various times in the future.

Results produced by this technique are typically highly quantitative. This technique is typically used to forecast developments such as the speed of operation, level of performance, cost reduction, improved quality, and operating efficiency.

Fisher-Pry Analysis is a mathematical technique used to project the rate of market adoption of technically superior new technologies and, the corresponding loss of market share by old technologies.

The technique is based on the fact that the adoption of such new technologies normally follow a pattern known by mathematicians as the "Logistic Curve." This adoption pattern is defined by two parameters. One determines the time at which adoption begins, and the other determines the rate at which adoption occurs. These parameters are determined from early adoption data, and the resulting pattern is used to project the time at which market penetration reaches any given level.

Results produced by this technique are highly quantitative. The technique forecasts how the installed base of telecommunications equipment changes over time, how rapidly a new chemical production process is adopted, and the rate at which digital measuring devices replace analog devices in petroleum refineries, etc.

Gompertz Analysis is very similar in concept to Fisher-Pry Analysis, except that it better models adoptions driven by technical superiority. However, customers suffer no significant penalty for late adoption of the new technology. Like Fisher-Pry analysis, Gompertz analysis projects adoption by use of a two parameter mathematical model. Early adoption is used to determine these parameters and the resulting adoption curve. Results are highly quantitative, and the technique is often used to project adoption of consumer products such as high-definition television, digital camcorders, new automobile features, etc.

Growth Limit Analysis utilizes a mathematical formulation known as the Pearl Curve to project the pattern in which maturing technologies approach development limits. This is useful to organizations in analyzing maturing technologies, in setting feasible research goals, and in determining the additional development spending. The technique is also be useful in determining if new technical approaches might used to overcome apparent technical limits.

Learning Curve Techniques are based on the fact that, as more and more items of a given type are produced, the price of production tends to decrease at a predictable rate.

For example, each doubling of a particular item might result in a cost reduction of 15%. In some cases, key technical parameters improve in a similar pattern. The learning curve phenomenon is reflected as a straight line on log-log graph paper, which makes projection relatively simple. Results are highly quantitative. The technique is used to set price and technical performance targets for developing technologies, particularly in the middle stages of development.

Pattern Finders

Pattern Finders believe that the future reflects a replication of past events. Powerful feedback mechanisms in our society, together with basic human drives, cause future trends and events to occur in identifiable cycles and predictable patterns. Thus, one can best address the future by identifying and analyzing analogous situations from the past and relating them to probable futures.

Analogy Analysis is based on the observation that the patterns of technical development and market capture for new technologies are often similar to those for like technologies. In applying this technique, forecasters identify appropriate analogies and analyze both similarities and differences.

It is desirable to identify more than one applicable example in order to minimize the probability of selecting false or inappropriate analogies. The results are typically semi-quantitative in nature, and are often presented as a range of possibilities rather than a single projection.

Precursor Trend Analysis takes advantage of the constant lag period between the development of a technology and the subsequent creation of another related development. For example, the first application of technical advances in passenger cars typically occurs four to five years after application in racecars. Similarly, the application of new technologies in commercial products follows laboratory demonstration by a relatively constant period.

One can project the status of the lag technology at some future date by observing the status of the lead technology. This technique also allows the extension of lag technology forecasts by building on forecasts of lead technologies. Results from using this technique are usually highly quantitative.

Morphological Matrices provide a formal method for uncovering new product and process possibilities. In applying this technique, users first determine the essential functions of the product or process and the different ways to satisfy them. They use the matrix to identify new, reasonable combinations of these that result in practical new products or processes. Results are qualitative in nature. The technique is used to identify non-obvious new opportunities for a company. It may also show products and processes that competitors are developing or considering.

Feedback Models provide a way to account for the interactions that connect technical, economic, market, societal, and economic factors as the future unfolds. In using this technique computer models are developed that mathematically specify the relationships between each of the relevant factors. For example, advances in technology may result in improved products for increased sales. This may result in more funds for further advance in technology. The results of this technique are highly quantitative, but are often used to examine qualitative consequences of trends, events, or decisions. The technique is most commonly used to formulate high-level strategies or policy.

Market Shapers

If the future is determined by the strategic intent, beliefs and actions of various individuals, organizations, and institutions, it is susceptible to modification and change by these entities. Consequently, the future is protected by examining the stated and implied goals of decision-makers and trendsetters, evaluating how they affect future trends and events, and determines the long-term results.

Impact Analysis provides a simple, formal method for integrating the fact that, in a complex society such as ours, trends, events, and decisions often have consequences that are neither intended nor foreseen. The technique combines the use of left-brain and right brain thinking to project the secondary, tertiary, and higher order impacts and implications of such occurrences. Results are qualitative in nature. The technique is often used to analyze potential consequences of projected technical advances or to determine the direction of forecasting efforts.

Content Analysis is founded on the concept that the relative importance of social, political, commercial and economic issues are reflected by the amount of media attention the issue receives. By measuring, over time, changes in such factors as column-inches in newspapers, time allocated on television, and, more recently, number of hits on the internet, forecasters can project the direction, nature, and rate of change. In the technical arena, this technique is used to project advances in new technologies, as well as growing market attraction. The results of this technique are often displayed in a quantitative format, but are typically used only for qualitative analysis.

Stakeholders' Analysis is a formal method examining the influence that various individuals and institutions have on future developments. It explicitly identifies those people and organizations, internal and external that have a "stake" in particular decisions, projects, or programs. It analyzes the importance that each individual or group assigns to these issues; and the relative influence they have on developments. Results from this technique are normally semi-quantitative. The technique is often used to test the validity of forecasts that are impacted by unexpected opposition or support.

Patent Analysis is based on the presumption that increased interest in new technologies, and conviction of their practicality and appeal, is reflected in increased R&D activity. This is reflected by increased patent activity. Consequently you can both identify new technology opportunities and assess the state of development of given technologies by analyzing the pattern of patent application in appropriate fields. Results from the application are often presented in quantified terms but their use in decision-making is normally qualitative.

Flexible Adapters

If the future results from a series of events and actions that are essentially unpredictable and, to a large extent, random, and identifying a wide range of possible trends and events, carefully monitoring developments in technical and social environments provides insight and a high degree of planning flexibility.

Scanning, Monitoring, and Tracking techniques are founded on the observation that, for most new technologies, a finite, often considerable, amount of time is required to bridge the gap between conception and commercialization. If you are alert, you can discern changes in technology, market, and other business factors in time to take maximum advantage of them.

All three techniques are employed to identify and evaluate developments that might materially impact your organization's operations and strategies. Although the three techniques are similar in many respects, they do differ in purpose, methodology, and degree of focus.

- Scanning seeks to identify any trend or event that might impact the organization and is, therefore, by design, essentially unfocused.
- Monitoring follows general trends in specified areas and is, thus, more focused than scanning.
- Tracking follows developments in a limited area and is, consequently, highly focused.

Results from each of these techniques vary between highly quantitative to basically qualitative. Generally, results are less quantitative in scanning activities and more quantitative in tracking activities.

The Alternate Scenarios technique provides a structured method for integrating a number of individual forecasts into a series of comprehensive, feasible narratives about how the future might develop. It provides a format that allows you to relate the implications of various forecasts. The results from this technique range from highly quantitative to purely qualitative depending on the objectives of the effort, its organization, and purposes. This technique assists you in critical decision-making. Although a single scenario can be used for making decisions, the use of a series of alternate scenarios allows executives to take account of the fact that the future is never projected with certainty. It helps determine how appropriate flexibility is built into plans.

Monte Carlo Models are computer models that take explicit account of the fact that all projections of future trends and events are based upon probability. In this technique, all of the steps involved in the development of a new technology are identified, and their inter-relationships specified in a mathematical model. Numerical values are assigned to the probability of each event occurring in various ways and the length of time these events will take. The model is then run many times to determine the probability of various outcomes. The results of the technique are highly quantitative, and projects technology development times and patterns, allocate resources and track the development of emerging technologies.

Intuition Followers

Used when you believe a complex mixture of inexorable trends, random events, and the actions of key individuals and institutions shapes the future, intuition followers feel there is no rational technique that can be used to forecast the future. They gather as much information as possible and depend on subconscious information processing in the brain and personal intuition to provide useful insights on future trends and events.

The Delphi Survey technique is a method for taking advantage of the talent, experience and knowledge of a number of experts in a structured manner to exchange divergent views without direct confrontation. The technique involves initial projections, usually in quantitative terms, of future events. After the initial projections are correlated, participants are asked to explain, anonymously, their differences in a series of follow-up rounds. Results are normally semi-quantitative and the technique projects future technical, market, and other developments, to uncover fundamental differences of opinion and to identify non-conventional ideas and concepts.

Nominal Group Conferencing is a formal technique for structuring the input from a number of subject matter experts. The technique is similar in some ways to "brain-storming", but its structure requires all participants take active part in the process. It also requires participants to individually generate new ideas, to silently assess the ideas of others, to jointly examine the implications of new ideas with others and to formally evaluate a series of options. The results of this technique are typically semi-quantitative. Nominal Group Conferencing is often used to project future developments, to uncover new business opportunities, or to identify new solutions to old problems.

Structured and Unstructured Interviews are methods for gathering and correlating the thoughts and opinions of a collection of experts about how the future will unfold.

Structured Interviews are similar to traditional opinion polls in that the interviewers know ahead of time the information they are seeking and structure the interview to extract it as efficiently as possible. The use of personal interviews rather than written surveys promotes participation, decreases the probability of misinterpretation, and assists in assessing the qualification of participants. Results are typically quantitative in nature and are used to project such items as potential market size, rate of technical advance, and general business factors.

Unstructured Interviews are used when the subject area is not well defined. The interviewer begins each session with only a limited concept of how the interview is structured. Each question is based on the answer to the previous question. The interview is essentially free-form and results are either qualitative or semi-quantitative. This technique is particularly valuable in identifying key issues, clarifying general concepts, identifying additional experts and formulating future structured interviews and surveys.

Summary

The choice of the best forecasting method for any particular situation is really not a simple task. Sometimes more than one method is appropriate. The first issue you must address is whether many data points are available. If not, judgmental procedures are called for.

For judgmental procedures, you must determine whether the situation involves interaction among decision-makers and whether large changes are involved. For large changes, is policy analysis involved, and if so, what is the best source of evidence? If one has a large quantity of data, does this consist of time series data?

The next issue involves knowledge about the expected empirical relationships. For example, meta-analyses is done so that, in most situations, excellent prior knowledge exists about price elasticity. If empirical knowledge of relationships is available, use econometric models.

In addition, consider domain knowledge, such as your own knowledge about the situation. For time series situations where one lacks causal knowledge, extrapolation is appropriate. If there is no prior knowledge about relationship, but domain knowledge exists (such as if you know that sales will increase), use rule-based forecasting. If you do not have time series data or prior knowledge about relationships, analogies are appropriate if domain knowledge is lacking. The list is not comprehensive.

The conditions may not always be clear nor is the preceding comprehensive. Use different approaches to the problem and combine the forecasts. The forecasts from these approaches can then be combined. The nature of making innovative products and technologies sometimes make any forecast counterproductive of misplaced leads to overconfidence and insensitivity to elements of surprises. The most useful thing is your learning when marketers try to make sense out of the data and resolve important uncertainties to understand risks that your decisions lead to or away from. Accept and get comfortable with these uncertainties and focus on the very source of these uncertainties. In the end, marketing of innovative products and technologies is all about trying to fully understand and manage uncertainty.

CHAPTER 7

Promoting Consumer Adoption

Many innovative products are based on new technological developments or manufacturing processes and require customers to use them differently. These products either revolutionize existing product categories or define totally new one. Since innovative products represent "quantum leaps" compared to previously marketed technologies, they often warrant major changes to marketing and consumption systems.

Examples include digital videophones, the Segway human transporter, DVD, MP3, CD, SACD, digital photography, biometrics and HDTV and HD Radio technologies. If the new product differs dramatically from existing products (in terms of features or benefits) a new product category is created. Providers as well as consumers may fail to grasp the significance of this occurrence. When some IBM executives predicted that personal computers would never be widely used, they viewed them from the perspective of an existing product category (high speed computing devices). When many start-ups launched innovative web-based businesses they expected adoption. They were viewing the internet and PC from the perspective of the home appliances. This perceptual limitation contributed to many failures. Very often new uses create a completely new product category with significant growth potential. It does, however, require adoption strategy planning to ensure consumer adoption.

The incongruity between innovative new products and their associated product categories, affects the way consumers evaluate them. An inverted U-shape relationship exists between the level of incongruity between a product, its associated product category and favorable product evaluations. When the level of incongruity is very high, consumers tend to evaluate products unfavorably.

As a consequence, innovative products are likely to enter the market at an inherent disadvantage. They are likely to be viewed with doubt and skepticism when first introduced. Incongruity also affects how decision-making information is gathered and processed. When faced with extreme incongruity, consumers tend to limit their information search. Instead of seeking out more information, they activate an alternative product category. Novices (i.e. those unfamiliar with the product or product category) are more likely to use category-based (rather than piecemeal or attribute-based) processing than experts. Since category-based processing increases the level of incongruity, novices resist adopting innovative products more than experts.

Consider many e-commerce businesses, with viable businesses models and unique customer value propositions. Hype drove many players to enter the market too fast, causing them to lose sight of management principles. Just as the meteoric rise of e-commerce was grossly exaggerated, so too is the news of its death.

Internet technology is working to help companies interact with customers, provide improved access to information, improve operational efficiencies and grow customer relationships. As with the adoption of any new technology, this is a slow, error-prone process. Making technology work requires more than slick marketing. Consumers are loath to change their habits—even when the benefits seem obvious to technology enthusiasts. More often than not, new technology augments, rather than replaces, the existing one.

Consider the transition from AM radio to the technologically superior FM. After World War II, it was clear to industry participants that FM represented the future of radio. The number of FM radio stations tripled between 1946 and 1948, and the industry was bracing for a quick transition to FM. Consumers were, however, unwilling to give up their favorite AM stations—or pay an extra $15 for a dual AM-FM receiver. They were also unsure which standard would prevail. And while FM was technically superior, its advantages were not meaningful to most people. By 1949, FM radio lost steam and the number of FM stations declined while AM stations increased in numbers.

Ten years later, the development of higher-quality recording made the advantages of FM apparent to the average consumer, increasing its adoption rate. It took FM radio 40 years to surpass AM. The superior technology was ultimately adopted, but the process was long and treacherous. In spite of the FM victory, AM radio has not vanished; the two simply coexist. The scenario is being re-enacted as satellite XM radio attempts to entice customers into paying a monthly fee to enjoy a wide selection of radio stations at home or while travelling. The market is further complicated by the introduction of High Definition (HD) Radio—the last bastion of analog broadcast. Developed by iBiquity Digital, HD Radio transmits digital audio and data alongside existing AM and FM signals, allowing listeners to enjoy CD-quality music via FM and FM quality sound via AM. It is a long awaited technology that allows radio broadcasters to win back their eroded market and to compete with CDs, Kazaa, MP3s and satellite radio players.

The lesson? E-commerce prevails quickly when it has a clear edge or evolves along with existing technologies and when standards are being adopted.

While technology changes at "internet time", people don't change habits quickly, and require a compelling reason to do so. Understanding and managing consumer adoption is one of the key roles of marketing.

Consider online grocery offerings. Ordering groceries online requires advance planning and waiting at home for delivery. Pure-play online grocers like Webvan were ahead of their market. In the heart of Silicon Valley, at that time it seemed obvious that there would be sufficient demand for its friendly, timesaving service. Yet, adoption was slow and the company, locked into huge infrastructure investments, driven by the assumption of rapid adoption they finally had to shut down.

The demise of Webvan does not mean online grocery shopping is forever doomed. Ordering groceries online is still the right solution for some people, for some products, some of the time. The solution has to match the adoption rate, with a gradual increase in the number of people changing their behavior. A younger generation, seeking convenience, will be met by customer-serving grocers in a decade-long dance of service meeting needs, as online and offline options evolve side-by-side.

When the benefits are compelling and the service is targeted to the right customers, people do switch. For example, online trading has forever changed the brokerage industry. Today the entire trading process occurs online, providing compelling benefits to investors. The combination of fast execution, low-cost and rich information increases the speed of adoption of online trading. The service was targeted to technology-savvy, self-directed individuals and became a tremendous success.

The percentage of individual trades submitted online rose from 8% in 1996 to more than 50% in 2001 during the boom market period. In spite of the market declines and reduced trading volumes in technology stocks (which are often traded online), more than a quarter of all individual trades still take place online today.

Along with the adoption of online trading, many investors insist on having multiple ways to trade. Charles Schwab's "Clicks and Mortar" strategy recognized early on that the combination of branch offices, telephone and online trading is more powerful than either online or offline services alone. Branches reinforce the brand, breed trust and enable customers to reach Schwab on their own terms. For all the hype, e-commerce still accounts for just 1 or 2% of the retail trade in the United States. That's not bad for a technology that is just being commercialized. The foundations are laid; companies like Webvan taught businesses a useful lesson. Marketing new products is all about managing adoption.

Most innovative products are either manufactured using new technology (e.g. vacuum packaging of consumer perishables or digital storage of information for entertainment purposes) or offer new technologies to the consumer (e.g. use of electromagnetic waves to heat and cook food in a microwave oven). From a consumer's perspective, this poses two major potential problems:

-   Incompatibility with existing products or physical space for placement or user's habits and applications
-   Unknown risks that are perceived as high
-   Skepticism whether promised benefits are deliverable

Electric cars are an example of an innovative product which is incompatible with existing products and with customer needs and expectations. Electric cars are incompatible with existing introduced products (gasoline-powered cars) since they use an alternative fuel source. This requires installation of a special converter-charger in the consumer's home or garage for operation.

The adopters of this new product invest an additional $2,000 to install the converter-charger before using the cars. Incompatibility with consumer needs and expectations arises since more time is required to "refuel" electric cars versus gasoline-powered cars.

Expected mileage before the next refueling is also lower than expected.

Based on experience with gasoline-powered vehicles, consumers expect to spend no more than several minutes refueling at a service station. They also expect to drive a considerable distance (200 miles or more in many cases) before refueling is required. In contrast, the batteries that power electric cars require recharging every 60 miles or so, and recharging may take several hours. While incompatibility with previously introduced products is to be expected given the nature of innovative products, it impedes consumer adoption.

Microwave ovens are another good example of slow consumer adoption. When first introduced, no one had any idea of how to cook with the new appliance. Reheating leftovers or take-out food was the most commonly cited application. Homemakers accustomed to cooking with traditional ovens and had no idea of what to do with this appliance. There were few microwave cook books, no instructions for microwave cooking on most instant dinners and few classes on microwave cooking. Once again, consumer adoption was impeded.

Digital camera users were also faced with problems of storing, transferring and printing photographs. The new technology did not fit the established photo finishing and physical storage system, which was designed around traditional photography. Only recently, desktop photo printers, connecting cables and storage devices (memory sticks and cards etc.) have promoted more rapid consumer adoption of this technology.

Consumers often perceive new technologies and products as more risky. Past research shows that the perceived risk is a critical determinant of a consumer's willingness to buy a new product.

Of relevance to our discussion of innovative products are two complementary conceptualizations of perceived risk. The first distinguishes between performance and financial risk. Performance risk is the possibility that the product will malfunction or fail to deliver the desired or promised benefits. Financial risk refers to the potential monetary outlay associated with the initial purchase price as well as the subsequent maintenance costs of the product. Since innovative products have no history of use, consumers associate higher levels of performance risk with adoption. Limited data on actual product performance and limited experience with the product or product category are likely to cause consumers to experience greater uncertainty and risk.

Furthermore, new technologies are typically introduced in the market at very high prices. For example, when pocket calculators were first introduced, they sold for more than 50 times their current price as did digital video cameras, which sold for more than 15 times their current price. The old, more expensive digital cameras also camera weighed twice as much.

Even though pocket calculators represented a revolutionary new technology, the financial risk for early adoption was huge. This seriously limited the number of potential buyers purchasing these products at that time. Similarly, electric cars also are an innovative product whose adoption entails both performance and financial risk. Consumer experience with the product is negligible, leading to expectations of high performance risk, and with initial outlays of more than $30,000, substantial financial risk.

A second conceptualization of perceived risk is product related. The perceived risk consists of two basic subcategories: product-category risk, and product-specific risk.

Product-category risk is the risk inherent in purchasing a product while specific risk is associated with that item's product category. Consumers perceive the adoption of innovative products as high risk since many such products define new product categories. An innovative product may be the only representative in its product category. Consequently, all perceived product-category and product-specific risks would center on the new products.

Innovative Products Can Shape Market Structures

The introduction of innovative products alters market structure in a number of ways. Innovative products require new alliances and partnerships between different market players. This may change the competitive structure of the marketplace. Innovative product providers also develop complementary infrastructures to support the adoption and use of their products. Introduction of an innovative product also significantly alters the market structure. One of the key factors currently limiting the usefulness of electric cars is the battery —as it discharges rather quickly and is very bulky.

A more efficient battery would help all car manufacturers. It is in their common interest to develop a more efficient battery. This mutual goal has brought the three big competing automakers together to jointly sponsor the US Advanced Battery Consortium (USABC), supported by the Department of Energy and the utility-supported Electric Power Research Institute (EPRI). Together they are investing $260 million in battery research over a five-year period. Here, a common goal (the success of an innovative product) creates the conditions for competitors and adversaries to work together.

Digital photography basically redefines the competencies required to compete successfully. This is a giant shift for companies such as Kodak, Fuji and Polaroid. Overnight companies such as HP and Sony suddenly entered this market. Though Polaroid's "instant photography" was once the industry value proposition this big blue chip corporation has since been forced into chapter eleven.

Another example how innovative products shape industry structure is a Silicon Valley start-up called Moxi, which launched the Moxi Media Center, and Moxi Media Extension. The company designs software and hardware for cable and satellite set-top boxes. This lets them effectively function as digital entertainment centers.

With this innovative product, consumers send an email, download video, play games and perform other PC-like tasks on TV. The Moxi MC is a set-top box design using the company's

138

middleware, which runs between a modified version of the Linux operating system and interactive services, such as a digital video recorder, digital music jukebox, enhanced DVD playback. Online capabilities including instant messaging, e-mail, Web browsing and chat. It serves as the focal point for digital content in the home and wirelessly, or through wires, communicates with other consumer electronics devices, such as televisions, throughout the home. The set-top boxes based on Moxi MC software are designed to include a modem, hard drive and Firewire ports.

This essentially changes the competitive dynamics of two industries: television and computing. Moxi's software is added to EchoStar's advanced satellite television receivers. Microsoft, Intel, Apple Computer and major PC companies, are developing technology that bridges the gap between TV and computer technologies. Many of these attempts will fail.

Component costs, customer indifference and other factors douse the enthusiasm behind past interactive TV and earlier PC-TV experiments. Microsoft's eHome division expects to announce its goal of making PCs running Windows XP the entertainment center of the home. It is also introducing Mira, a handheld computing device that allows consumers to perform the same sort of tasks that Moxi enables. The battle here is between the TV, PC and Handheld Devices.

The transition from the old market structure to a new one may take some time. The consumer faces difficulties in this transition, which acts as a barrier to innovative product adoption.

For example, to support the recharging of electric cars, companies are planning to build a large network of recharging stations. A study conducted in Adelaide, South Australia, and reported by Payton (1995), indicated that the battery-recharging stations have to be as easily accessible as gasoline stations, to ensure the electric car's success. Obviously, such a network takes time to build, and the early adopters of the electric car would be at a disadvantage in terms of availability of recharging stations. This partial development of the market structure in the initial phase of an innovative product launch tends to hamper the adoption process.

Introduction of the compact disc (CD) also illustrates how innovative products can shift market structures. At the time of its introduction, the CD was a totally new product that set new standards in audio reproduction. It displaced vinyl records and to some degree audiocassette tapes (killing reel-to-reel and eight-track tapes which were already slowly becoming obsolete). It also changed the production and distribution in the audio entertainment industry. This provided the impetus for the development of new audio playback equipment and ancillary industries providing supplementary equipment such as changers, auto audio equipment, and portable playback devices. Retail outlets and suppliers changed layout and distribution to accommodate the CD display. They created a secondary packaging doubling the size of the CD boxes since consumers were used to flipping through the larger sized LP albums.

Alliances were formed between hardware and software providers, like Sony and NV Philips Polygram Records to ensure an adequate supply of software. Following widespread introduction, a frequent consumer complaint was lack of adequate software—The CD was an innovative product that set new standards. Many record manufacturers were not quick enough to release or re-release material in the new format.

The same occurred with the Video Laser Disc, an early digital videodisc format with the size of the disc same as the LPs. Now DVD faces the same challenges. However, with the lessons of past experience, DVD is hitting the mainstream in a relatively short period of time compared to previous launches of a new format. It is also experiencing much greater success. Now both Super Audio Compact Disc (SACD) and DVD Audio (DVDA) face the same kind of challenges.

Perceived Risks

Customers' perceived risk and uncertainty pose considerable barriers to adoption, even when the consumer evaluates and considers adopting an innovative product. Favorable attitudes are not converted to actual purchases without a "final push".

Surrogate buyers play a significant role in providing that extra impetus. Accountability in making recommendations reduces consumer uncertainty in that they have "expert endorsement" and an avenue for formal recourse should the product not meet their expectations.

Another barrier to adoption is limited availability of the innovative products. In the early stages of the product life cycle following market introduction, market structure is not fully developed, limiting availability and accessibility of innovative products. In these instances, surrogate buyers facilitate the adoption process by providing access to sellers/providers of innovative products.

Adoption of an innovative product at times involves major behavioral and lifestyle changes. Although an innovative product offers significant advantages over existing products, if consumers are not willing to make required lifestyle or behavioral changes, the innovative product has a slim chance of commercial success. It also is possible for consumers to overlook required behavioral changes. For example, Vermont offered its residents a really innovative electricity plan. Under this plan, residents are charged differential rates depending on what time of day (TOD) they consumed electricity. Rates were higher during peak consumption periods and lower during off-peak periods.

Adoption of this plan required making behavioral changes in order to take advantage of the differential rate structure. The TOD households changed the time they did laundry, prepared meals, and used water heaters. Households that elected to adopt the TOD rates without being aware of required behavioral changes quickly became disillusioned with the new rate plan and rejected it.

Innovative Products Require Consumers to Learn and Adapt

Innovative products require active consumer learning and significant cognitive investment up-front. They become aware, through information channels, of the product and its benefits. They also learn about innovative products through trial. Trial involves actual use of the product and occurs either prior to adoption (test driving an automobile or trying out digital video editing equipment at a electronics store) or following adoption (e.g. learning a new software package). Because learning is active and requires the acquisition and processing of product-related information, it is hindered when information pertaining to the innovative products is unavailable or difficult to comprehend. In either case, assimilation and internalization of information pertaining to innovative products requires consumer effort. Inaccessibility, for whatever reason, impedes the consumers' ability to learn, which reduces chances of adoption.

Conversely, in an age of information and "innovation overload" in which new products are continuously introduced, many innovative products providers attempt to provide consumers with as much information as possible about their product. Rather than stimulate learning, excessive information, by its sheer quantity and variety is also an impediment to learning, creating barriers to adoption. The result is often delayed purchase.

Although not readily apparent, post-adoption trial is a significant issue for consumer learning about innovative products. With innovative products, which require significant cognitive investment in post-adoption learning, consumers are resistant to adopt subsequent innovative products despite potential benefits due to the financial and time investments required by the existing product. Personal computers and software packages are examples of innovative products that fit this profile.

142

One interesting example is Microsoft's innovative iLoo. The company that gave us Windows, Word, Excel, and Tablet PCs has toyed with the idea to develop the first wireless-modem-and-computer-equipped portable toilet. The iLoo features six-channel audio surround sound, a plasma display, and a (waterproof) wireless keyboard. The potential seems endless. User can surf, send email, visit chat room, participate in on-line auctions and shop all from the comfort of your own portable toilet. There's even advertising potential being considered in such a water closet that includes looking for advertisers who want to put their URLs on toilet paper. Problem was, given what toilet paper is typically used for, will the average advertiser want their product associated with such behavior? And how long will it take for consumer to learn and adapt to multi-tasking in this usage environment?

Figure 7-1 An Example of Product Innovation That Requires User To Learn and Adapt

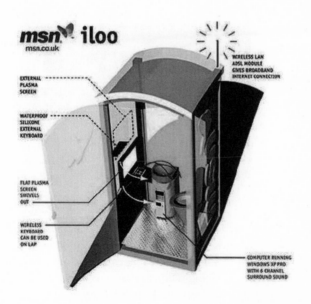

Innovative Products Induce Behavioral Changes

Adopters of innovative products are often required to significantly modify their behavior. Consider, for example, the behavioral changes required in adopting an innovative product like a videophone.

Mobility is restricted because users are required to face the camera while engaging in a conversation. Spontaneity is reduced on the part of both the caller and the receiver who might feel the need to "prepare" prior to engaging in conversation. Also, freedom to engage in other activities while chatting with friends is curtailed. There are several obstacles that innovative products providers must overcome to induce behavioral change. The most difficult one is changing user behavior.

Figure 7-2 An Example of Product Innovation That Requires User Behavioral Changes

Customers are seldom voluntary participants in things that signify major changes for them. Usually significant benefits entice them into adopting a new product. Current practices or routines are reluctantly changed. Habits constitute a psychological equilibrium between time-tested beliefs and devices used. Change requires a cognitive effort that the innovative products must justify. Habits are hard to overcome and sometimes go beyond simple utility. For example, some customers may choose a hairdresser more for his gossip and friendly chatter than his ability to style hair.

These broad symbolic needs are actually not easy to identify and certainly difficult to change. The complaints I often hear about the conservatism of consumers is mainly a reflection of their ignorance of cognitive psychology. Human beings are physiologically and psychologically limited and often have difficulty handling complexity. They resist change. Rather than pushing against the human grain, it is better to assess such resistance and adapt a product and its marketing accordingly.

Another reason for slow adoption is many technology-based products require the meeting of some preconditions that before mass adoption really occurs. One such precondition results from the fact that products become valuable when other people own and use them if compatibility is required. Economists called this "network externalities". For many technological products, this applies. Hence, adoption is slow until a product takes off. Momentum accelerates the pace of adoption. The rate depends on whether there are common standards being adopted or mandated by regulatory authorities. This creates enormous pressure on first movers to disseminate hardware in order to facilitate acceptance.

Buyers often resist the buying hardware until some clear standard emerges and they are confident about future availability of software and support at a competitive price.

This creates the paradox faced by companies such as Apple, Sun, Sony, Panasonic, 3Com and others. All hardware providers want to control profitable sales of software, and therefore resist endorsing any open standard. However, a nonproprietary standard cannot expect to earn extraordinary profits on basic hardware over the long run. In many cases, companies hope to appropriate above-average returns in the short run, before imitation occurs, or in the sale of complementary software.

One company that based its business strategy on this idea is D&M Holdings. The company plays on convergence on the high-end home entertainment market by acquiring a host of audio-video brands that merge the worlds of digital convergence and audiophilia. They now own Denon, Marantz, McIntosh (all three are high-end players with strong brand names and heritages), Replay TV hard disc, Escient music and video servers and Rio portable music players. They are making their entire product family network convergence-ready. The first big product launch is a new Denon server, which holds every piece of D&M technology. It can store 1,000 CDs' worth of music on two 129-gigabyte hard drives and has a video recorder built-in. It can send DVD-quality video to a maximum of four TVs at 6 to 9 megabits per second. Rather than compressing music from a CD, a process that lowers the sound quality, the server uses a new standard from Mediabolic, another start-up that D&M has invested in to store and transmit music uncompressed. Ultimately it allows users to burn their own DVDs of shows and movies. It's much easier that storing music and videos on the PC.

Another barrier facing some technology products is the difficulty in arranging product trials. With consumer products and goods, features or functionalities are demonstrated through in-store or TV demonstrations. Software, be it games or business applications, often offer free trial software available for instant download. However, for many innovative products that require integration or installation, it is still a key barrier since the consumer cannot engage in any actual product trial. Examples include on-board GPS systems, home music servers and XM satellite radios for automobiles. All require custom installation and need to be tested beyond the showroom.

Figure 7-3 Technologies Adoption Rate Comparison

Technology	Year of Introduction	Penetration Level After 15 Years (%)
Clothes Washer	1908	23
Refrigerator	1911	3
Air Conditioner	1932	1
Microwave Oven	1957	1
Vacuum Cleaner	1908	33
Radio	1920	72
Color TV	1954	38
ATMs	1970	60
Videoconference	1981	10
DVD	1998	81 *
Digital Camera	1999	87 *
Digital Video Recorder	2000	64 *
Satellite Radio	2002	43 *

* Estimates

Innovative technology-based products must be correctly positioned and differentiated. The newer the technology, the better the chance to achieve first mover advantages and a higher level of differentiation. Yet this also increases the chance of having a retarded market adoption. The newer the idea or the more "discontinuous" the technology, the more likely for such scenario to happen.

It often makes more sense to integrate innovative products and technologies into something consumers are already familiar with. It is a highly difficult task to convince a consumer that a product is so unique and innovative that it is in a category by itself. If the innovative product is positioned as a substitute, it must a "superior substitute". It can either expand the functions or deliver increased customer benefits. Is the product fundamentally unique? Is there a compelling reason for customers to switch to this new innovative product?

The key is minimizing consumer disruption. The less disruption, the greater the likelihood of rapid adoption. When it is difficult and it does not make sense to relate the new innovative products to existing categories, the best alternative is to make the technology as invisible as possible and emphasize only its unique functions or special capabilities.

Mercedes Benz has used this strategy. Almost all technological innovations implemented over the years are very subtle and somewhat hidden. The overall interior panel design remains almost the same and switches and controls are kept to a minimum. Buyers simply know that Mercedes Benz is so well engineered that technological innovations are under the hood and intuitively operated.

There are some cases where an innovative product with radical technologies needs differentiation based on its breakthrough features. A common mistake is presenting too many messages, covering all product attributes. This simply confuses the buyer and reduces the probability and scope for adoption. While most innovative products have worthwhile attributes, is important to focus on the one that is most important to the user.

Pricing innovative products is also very tricky. Traditionally, companies recovered the development cost as early as possible by adopting a "skimming" strategy". Prices for products were very high in the beginning and then lowered them in line with manufacturing costs as certain scale was reached. A drawback to this strategy is that it allows potential market entrants to watch, and jump in and establish a large user base at a lower price.

The innovator remains product leader and continues to introduce high-end models with unique features. Innovation is very difficult to maintain today because of growing competition between alternative technologies. Customers want the new functionality an innovative product has to offer but are only willing to pay a very small premium. Making the innovative products affordable within a very short period of time becomes a key challenge. As does creating a large enough demand for a new product. An alternative is to share the risks with the early adopters or in some cases eliminate high up-front costs. Many companies resort to offering financial leasing for business users and some use a pay for performance approach.

Almost every industry has unique characteristics as well as disparate groups of early adopters. To have innovative new products accepted early and widely, find the most receptive segments and bring in others on board quickly. Here's how:

- Identify the broad segment or segments most receptive to the new products in terms of their buying criteria and process;
- Identify the most receptive buyer within those segments and get to know more about their needs and the perceived risks to this new product. Try to neutralize those risks;
- Build success case studies from early adopters and communicate them to the mass market.

Figure 7-4 Technologies Diffusion Modeling

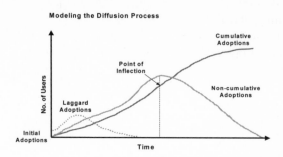

Summary

There are a number of implications if you market innovative products. Though such products are often not treated separately from other new products (such as product extensions) the process is significantly different.

The unique characteristics of innovative products provide opportunities as well as challenges. These products define or significantly modify existing product categories so potential adopters must be educated about the features and advantages. Non-technical and easy-to-understand language should be used to enhance consumer comprehension.

Since these products fulfill some needs consumers are unaware of (as was the case when computers were first introduced), you must bring these latent needs to a conscious level.

The other key to success is to be flexible enough to capture the ever-evolving needs of early adopters. An open mind and a high degree of flexibility in terms of what "product" is offered as well as "how" and "when" are critical. Managing adoption is best seen as a combination of market discovery and demand creation.

CHAPTER 8

Brand Taxonomies

Branding has become almost a religion in some corporations, and is difficult to dislodge, because many believe that the brand itself is something that changes consumer behavior. What do we mean by "the brand" in today's marketplace? The general consensus is that the brand means the business.

The business is not a reflection of a mission statement made in a vacuum, the business is a reflection of everyone affecting its performance in the marketplace: its employees, allies, suppliers and consumers. The brand effectively represents the culture of all who touch the business. The brand is not a singular thing. There are multiple touch points in the entire chain of creation. A brand is a product or a group of products, service or a group of services or a corporate name.

Each creates different dynamics on how a business manages the brand. We tend to think that branding comes first and company success follows. In fact, it's the exact opposite. Companies should develop their products first, and build the channel and service delivery infrastructures. Then their brand evolves along with the success of the products over time.

The traditional thinking around branding was to endow a commodity with unique characteristics through the creative use of name, slogan, packaging and advertising. However, in a world where there is a muddle of images and messages, it is increasingly difficult for a brand to rise above the noise to be noticed and remembered. A more sophisticated and strategic concept of brand is needed.

The proliferation of media (specialty channels, the internet, wireless applications) has seriously diluted the effectiveness of traditional forms of brand building. Add to this the increasing interest in understanding brand equity and what sort of development (marketing, quality improvements) augments equity, and it becomes clear that you need to develop more sophisticated tools for measuring how specific marketing activities form customer impressions of the brand and add value to the brand.

CEOs must sell the marketing department's vision to the rest of the company and help build brand consensus and understanding at all levels. Brand management is becoming a team-based activity, undertaken by senior managers from different disciplines and backgrounds. While this results in a more experienced team, the nature of the brand may differ between individuals due to large quantities of information presented and different perceptual processes. Brand taxonomies can be very useful tools for surfing diversity among the brand's team, and help achieve a more coherent implementation of brand strategy. Brand taxonomies use a process to identify and resolve diversity among the brands' team.

Brands are also used to align an organization's people and resources around its business goals. An organization's fiscal responsibility and its ability to keep the business competitive, rely on the people that determine its direction and its operation. As a brand's success is ultimately linked to its financial performance, it's imperative that brand accountability emerges from those responsible for performance. Here are a few insights:

- Sponsorship and active participation at the executive level give credence to the brand as a business. Demonstration and reinforcement of the vision should come from the CEO. There must be a brand champion, a role model that promotes employee cooperation and understanding. The CEO's responsibility is to become the evangelist and storyteller of the brand. Cooperation among the CEO, the senior executive team, the businesses within the organization and the cross-functional teams, make a brand successful in the market.
- Actively aligning the company's day-to-day operation in accordance with the business' culture and vision ensures that the brand promise is met from top to bottom. Operationalization of the brand through alignment of people, processes, technology, and systems results in delivery on the brand promise and experience. All departments from sales to customer support lay claim to the brand and understand their role in promoting it.

The process of building and sustaining brands is changing. From the early 1960's to the early 1990s, it was undertaken primarily by junior brand managers, who focused on tactics, regarded their posts as good training grounds and moved on to more senior marketing roles after a short tenure.

With harsher business environments forcing firms to work harder to deliver shareholder value, a shift is occurring in the way firms are organized around brand management. Firms are now restructuring around customers and the processes that add value to customers' total experiences such as customer relationship management and interactive marketing management. This has led to brand management becoming more of a team-based activity, managed at more senior levels, by people who adopt a more strategic perspective. This brings a broad spectrum of skills to address the myriad of company-wide issues implementing brand strategy presents. However, because of team members' diverse backgrounds, there is a great difference in interpretations about the nature of their brand. In situations like this, firms might not gain maximum benefit from harmonizing all the activities across their value chains, since different departments have the same goal. This chapter illustrates how different categories of brands need to be managed in very different ways.

Unless all members of the brand's team fully appreciate the type of brand and assets that they are managing, they may individually be making different and inconsistent assumptions about the work their department should undertake. At best, this engenders sub-optimal efficiency.

For example, one organization launched a successful shampoo brand. A few years later an up-marker variant was added to the product line. The nature of this new brand variant was poorly communicated internally, and consequently some of the national accounts sales team adopted an inappropriate policy of price discounting to gain distribution through some of the major pharmacies. When the firm undertook an audit to assess the variant's poor performance, they recognized the need for a brand taxonomy that facilitated internal communication about the nature of their different brands, and which helped develop a more coherent brand strategy.

Different categories of brands need different management approaches. A process enables members of the brand's team to recognize differences in perceptions, and encourages a more coherent approach to brand management.

Why diverse views among the brand's team? In part, different views result from the large amount of brand information team members review and digest. Managers' perceptual processes, which vary widely between individuals and departments, also create diversity. Rapid convergence makes it difficult to define what categories the product belongs to and to place brands within those categories.

Brand information deluge managers are presented with large quantities of information about their firm's brands. These come from a variety of sources including brand reviews, market research reports, the sales force, promotions agencies and distributors. Yet our finite cognitive capabilities only cope with a limited amount of information. One of the many ways to cope is to simplify, using mental models that contain sufficient information, without all the complex details. For example, a manager working in a firm with a portfolio of brands might simplify by mentally categorizing the large number of brands into a small number of groups, based on their perceived similarity.

Through drawing inferences, based on each group's characteristics, brand appreciation and understanding grows. One of the problems is that, because of team members' backgrounds, different simplification processes are used. While one brand manager may categorize his brands based on the production processes employed or features included, another may group according to different distribution channels or customer segments. As a consequence, there is always a scope for diverse perceptions between the brand and the marketing team.

Understanding Managers' Perceptual Processes

A consideration of perceptual processes provides further explanation for diverse views. The type of information to which managers are exposed affects their views. With the team consisting of individuals from different departments, in addition to external advisers, it is unlikely that everyone has equal access to all the firm's internal information. Further affecting their views about their brand, different individuals also read different magazines and attend diverse trade conferences.

When reading about your firm and competitors' brand marketing activity, you may have become virtually conditioned to accepting the historical strategies followed by individual brands. Small deviations may not be noted. For example a competitor's brand, which has always been 12% cheaper than your brand, becomes 15% cheaper. Such a change, though potentially significant, may fall beneath the reader screen. When circulated with brand documentation, different managers are more likely to notice such a change. People are attentive to information that supports their prior beliefs and dismissive of information that contradicts their beliefs. Thus, even when the brand's team is given the same information, individuals focus on particular parts and their interpretations are tinged by personal biases. This is very common in real life.

Figure 8-1 Boundaries of Brand Strategy

A further hurdle is presented by the differences in comprehension between team members. When marketing, for example, innovative products and technology-based brands, some of the less technically-oriented managers may not wish to ask for clarification of a particular term, and selective comprehension could cause different interpretations. Another instance could be a section of a brand-planning document that is ambiguously phrased.

Even if everyone understands all the information in a brand's documentation, differences in memory retention rates can pose a problem. People's recall of information varies and this further compounds the possibility of different views between managers about the nature of their brand.

By definition, each brand strives to be different. Furthermore, because successful firms capitalize on their core competences, it is not unusual for a firm to have several different brands satisfying different niches in a market. Unless the entire brand team appreciates the differential characteristics of each brand in their portfolio, activities cannot be harmonized to reap the full advantage from coherent leverage of resources and skills across the value chain. In view of the preference people have for simplification, learning the nuances of each individual brand may not be productive. Instead, it may be helpful to get managers to appreciate where their brands fall on simple brand taxonomies. Once there is consensus among the team about how each of their brands is categorized, you can identify the most appropriate way to direct the activities of different departments.

Using Brand Taxonomies

There are a variety of ways to categorize brands. For example:

- How they're positioned to stress functional (think) or representational (feel) needs (FCB)
- How they achieve their leadership position (DMB&B)
- The balance between brand vitality and brand stature (Young and Rubicam)
- How a brand is used within the context of corporate strategy (Idris Mootee)

The strength of these taxonomies is that they enable you to appreciate brands and facilitate the identification of appropriate strategies to maintain or change the brand. The brand taxonomy arising from the functional/representational matrix was previously explained, along with empirical validation in low and high involvement sectors. Basically most brands are characterized by using the functionality representational matrix.

However, there are a number of brands that have a notable third dimension, (i.e. centrality value) which make other taxonomies more suitable. These brands adopt a strong view about the world, and they are concerned with stressing opinions. Body Shop, Timberland, Ben and Jerry and Benetton are good examples of brands with a notable centrality value dedicated to making people aware of social problems.

Refreshingly new taxonomies have recently been devised by two advertising agencies and, in view of their potential power, should be considered. Two new taxonomies have been developed on a proprietary basis, to help produce more effective advertising for their clients, through a better understanding of brands. I developed the fourth one for my strategy and marketing consulting firm on a proprietary basis. It helps companies look at brands from a corporate strategy perspective. However, all three taxonomies are based on a significant amount of qualitative and quantitative research, covering a wide spectrum of sectors. All are appropriate for low and high involvement purchasing situations.

DMB&B's Leadership Equity Model

Market share and profitability are strongly related. In the quest for high profits, organizations strive for brand leadership. In view of this, DMB&B undertook qualitative and quantitative market research into leading brands in the USA, the UK and Europe (DMB&B, 1994). Their research identified four categories of brands, defined by the type of relationship the brand leader had established with its consumers. The four categories are:

> - **Power Brands** inspiring rational trusts through excellence in product and service performance (Tide, Intel, IBM, Gillette, Costco, Duracell, Wal-Mart).

157

- **Identity Brands** facilitating character recognition, through association with the brand's personality. Examples include Levi's, Virgin, Martha Stewart, and Target etc.
- **Explorer Brands**, enabling consumers personally to develop through challenges and possibilities (Microsoft, Google, eBay, MasterCard, Disney, Landrover, Accenture).
- **Icon Brands** creating myths that consumers dream about sharing (McDonald, Nike, Coca Cola, BMW, Sony, Apple).

This categorization enables the competitive nature of brands in a market to be identified. For example, extending their work, airline brands can be categorized as:

- Lufthansa (power brand);
- Virgin Airlines (identity brand);
- Qantas Airways (explorer brand);
- Singapore Airlines (icon brand).

It also enables a firm to better understand its portfolio of brands. For example, it could be argued that for British Airways brand strategies are:

- BA First Class (power brand);
- BA Club World (identity brand);
- BA World Traveler (explorer brand);
- BA Concorde (icon brand).

Power brands, for example Fairy Liquid and Duracell, need continual R&D investment and high quality standards to ensure they always lead in delivering required benefits. Communications campaigns center on the "product as hero", dramatically demonstrating how superior the brand is at satisfying consumers' rationally evaluated, functional needs. Market research studies focus on regularly tracking competitors' performance and changes in consumers' evaluation criteria can enable fine-tuning of the brand's functional capabilities. Identity brands, such as Martha Stewart and Virgin Airways grow through well-established brand personalities.

Identity brands rapidly overcome consumers' choice dilemmas between functionally similar brands, by enabling consumers to recognize, "This is who I am; I feel much more comfortable with this brand". American Express, with their campaign "It says a lot about the real me" is an identity brand. These brands thrive when their personalities are subtly updated to reflect societal changes (e.g. "Steven" in Dell's "Dude" commercial).

Explorer brands strive to be at the edge of social (Nike, Body Shop, Timberland) and technological (Microsoft and Intel) advances. They are agents of change, supported by very flexible organizational structures that respond rapidly to indicators of new trends (e.g. Swatch, Sony, Nokia). They appeal to early innovators who are attracted by advertising showing how they can personally develop with these brands.

Icon brands have grown by associating themselves with a particular dream. This could be nostalgia, culture, fantasy or moral ideals. Advertising is key in supporting these brands. The challenge for brand strategists is to find ways to extend the dream and ensure functional excellence. Examples include Apple's "Think Different" campaign that honors many of the creative geniuses who have changed the world. The campaign celebrates the soul of the Apple brand—that creative people with passion can change the world for the better.

Figure 8-2 Young and Rubicam's Brand Asset Valuator

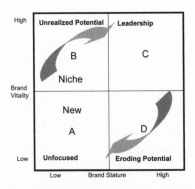

Young and Rubicam's Brand Asset Valuator

Another useful way to categorize brands is the use of Young and Rubicam Brand Asset Valuator. This brand typology has evolved out of Young & Rubicam's (Y&R's) worldwide study to understand how brands are built (Young & Rubicam, 1994).

They argue that brands evolve through four stages, i.e. differentiation to relevance then esteem followed by familiarity. Once launched, the primary objective is to differentiate the brand, to establish a distinctive, unique presence that attracts new users. To retain consumers, the brand needs to ensure it remains relevant to customer needs. In the fight against competitors, work is then needed to build the brand's esteem; ensuring consumers have a high regard for its capabilities. If the brand successfully overcomes these three hurdles, it achieves familiarity by becoming well established.

Applying this to the grocery retailing market, the declining independent retailers are failing to go beyond the differentiation stage. The garage forecourt retailers and 7 Eleven satisfy consumers through branding at the relevance stage, Gateway struggles at the esteem stage and Marks & Spencer thrives at the familiar stage. While this evolutionary typology helps brand strategists think about time-based planning, a more revealing categorization considers the relationships between the four phases.

Y&R's empirical analysis indicated that the strength of a brand, its "brand stature", is a combination of its esteem and familiarity scores. Its growth potential, or "brand vitality", is assessed from its differentiation and relevance scores. Once a brand's characteristics have been computed on these two dimensions, they are plotted on a two-dimensional matrix, as shown here. By examining where brands lie on this matrix, some of their strategic characteristics are appreciated, along with guidelines for future actions.

A brand begins life in quadrant A. By building the brand's differentiation and relevance; it grows to quadrant B. Then there are

160

two options, i.e. maintain themselves as niche brands, or invest in building the brand's esteem and encourage growth into quadrant C.

The top right hand quadrant is home to leading brands. By maintaining the brand's stature and creatively managing its vitality, the brand looks forward to a longer or extended lifetime. However, without sufficient maintenance of the brand's vitality, its differentiation and relevance decline, resulting in the brand increasingly selling on price promotions and declining to quadrant D. Some firms then lose confidence, cutting marketing support. This result in familiarity and esteem sinking, end the life of the brand as it is drained and disappears out of quadrant A.

This categorization is particularly helpful in brand planning. Where the brands are positioned, gives insight into resource allocation, (for example whether a maintenance or growth strategy is envisaged and which aspects of the brand, e.g. differentiation, relevance, etc.) required attention over the short and long term.

By plotting competitors' brands and tracking their movements, you learn whether competitors are growing stronger or weaker. This helps in the formulation of both defensive and attacking strategies. When considering extending the brand into new markets, it provides a succinct analysis of the competitive structure of that market and shows potentially attractive gaps.

For example, a 1994 analysis of the UK retail banking market showed the major players as being brands with high brand stature, but low brand vitality. The only financial services brand with any potential for growth was First Direct. This firm appeared to be aiming for the unoccupied top half of the brand vitality dimension. First Direct's success is partly due to the brand's representation of a clear set of values, which enables consumers to rapidly assess whether they feel comfortable associated with it. Most financial services brands draw heavily on corporate brand names, with little work to instill or project a clear set of ideals at the corporate level.

Based on a survey of more than forty-five thousand people across nineteen countries, Young & Rubicam makes a rather startling claim. In its Brand Asset Valuator 2001 report, the firm asserts that brands have taken on a godlike status: consumers often find greater meaning in them and the values they espouse than in religion.

As Conor Dignam reports in Ad Age Global, the study claims that superbrands like Calvin Klein, Gatorade, Ikea, Microsoft, MTV, Nike, Virgin, Sony PlayStation, and Yahoo can therefore also be called "belief brands." Although Dignam argues against the idea that consumers would treat brands as gods (because they will not be dictated to by them), he does accept the implications of the argument and make a different analogy. Brands, he says, are more like "best friends," in that they are an important part of people's lives, carry specific meanings for the consumer, and are respected or rejected based on how well they keep their promises.

Whether one calls them gods or "best friends," brands have clearly started to take on greater importance in consumers' lives. In fact, they have gone from objects with identity to identities in the guise of objects. The trend has gone so far, in fact, that people are beginning to speak the language of brands and even market themselves as brands.

Figure 8-3 Idris Mootee's Brand Life Cycle Model

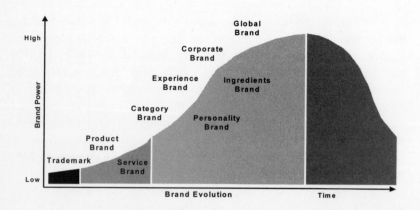

Idris Mootee's Brand Life Cycle Model

This is a model I developed in the mid 1990's to help companies understand how a particular brand should be positioned and its relation to the company's overall strategy.

This was based on an extensive study of US and European companies and their brands in different categories. This model enables companies to look at their corporate strategies, portfolio of brands and products in a meaningful way.

The analogy is that all brands basically evolve through four stages. Most of them start as a **Product Brand**, and then some are transformed into a **Service Brand**. Over years of brand building effort and market presence they gradually become either a **Category Brand**, which is defined as having leading market share within a category; or a **Personality Brand**, which establishes a strong brand personality that consumers identify with; or an **Experience Brand**, which goes beyond traditional service and product excellence with a strong sense of uniqueness.

Procter & Gamble is not particularly well known among consumers, while its brands—Ariel, Tide, Pampers, Always, Pantene are all very well known brands within their respective categories. Another type of brand is an **Ingredient Brand**, which is actually a co-brand since it co-exists together with others who might be responsible for physically manufacturing products or delivering of the service.

Ingredient Brands usually serve the purpose of providing additional trust or confidence and often signify the use of an exclusive or proprietary technology.

Examples include Lycra, Polartec, Gortex, Windows, Intel, Dolby and Oracle etc. This is the exact opposite of product brands. By contrast, the technology products communicate at the level of the company whose credibility and expertise have turned its name into a brand is stressed. The most successful case is likely Intel. If you buy an IBM computer today (already a powerful brand name), you will find two other co-brands: Windows and Intel. Twenty years ago we would not have envisioned the operation system and chip supplier would put their brand side by side with IBM. Today, however, they are top household names.

Ingredient Brands are not new. Only the term is. It existed hundred of years ago in the form of country brand. Remember all those "Made in Germany" and "Made in Japan" labels, symbolizing quality and sound engineering. The chemical and pharmaceutical industries have also become skilled in using the Ingredients Brand. When Du Pont differentiates its elasthane it becomes a symbol of quality. Without the Lycra label, consumers might believe that this fabric was a lower quality material. Lycra gave Du Point so much market power that the whole industry paid premium prices for this material. Du Pont actually made Lycra fashionable; how often have you heard of a chemical company who provides the material that has an impact of fashion trend.

After being extremely successful these brands become cash generating trademarks. They will then sometimes be moved up one level and become a **Corporate Brand** (the brand name becomes the corporation) or a **Global Brand**, expanding geographically to become a global dominant leader.

These different stances illustrate the major strategic choices required by each corporation, namely the optimum level at which a brand should be positioned to capture and create shareholder value. Companies sometimes can successfully move brands to different strategic levels and become the overall brand if that brand is very successful.

The British 4by4 motor company Rover produces the high end SUV Range Rover and Land Rover was once only a product brand. Land Rover now becomes the brand for the entire company. A recently launched smaller version is called Land Rover Freelander. Sometimes a brand needs to move from one category and become a brand of multi-categories. This is particularly common in fast moving consumer goods. In choosing a branding level you position against future competition to enjoy the best competitive advantage vis-à-vis channel partners and consumers. This is always the key consideration governing the choice of level.

The model suggests that the ultimate goal for all companies is to have a global brand. A strong global brand is a powerful weapon. These days, it is an indispensable one, as the economy challenges our faith in brands to deliver a profit.

According to Interbrand's "World's Most Valuable Brands 2000" study, for example, although Amazon's share price has declined, its brand value has increased by 233%. On the other hand, international power player Coca-Cola, although still the world's No.1brand, saw its value drop by 13%.

Technology brands did quite well—Microsoft, IBM, Intel, and Nokia placed second through fifth—not foreshadowing the precipitous crash in their stock prices about half a year after the study findings were released. Interbrand's second annual study of this kind reveals not only that global brands are "stable assets," but also that the most valuable brands are global. In fact to have a billion-dollar brand, a company has no other choice than to go global.

Management Implications

We realize that it is likely that members of a brand's team have differing perceptions about the nature of their brand. Since these managers direct staff in different departments, it is wise to evaluate disparity among the brand's team.

One way to recognize diversity is to run a workshop at which there is a review session, reminding managers about the brand taxonomy they adhere to. If there is no accepted taxonomy within the firm, the workshop should first describe some of the taxonomies and, through debate, gain consensus as to which taxonomy all the managers prefer to employ.

Leave each manager with notes and worksheets explaining the brand categorization process. Then remind the team of the key competing brands and ask them to individually categorize, on a sheet of paper, their brand and competitors' brands. Key competitors' brands are included since, due to simplification processes reviewed earlier; some managers find it easier to do this exercise thinking about clusters of brands rather than in isolation.

The team is then asked to write a few lines stating the strategy for their brand and the way their department is implementing it. These sheets are passed to the workshop leader, who arranges to have a summary table produced showing the nature of the firm's brand and the strategy or the brand plan, and how each manager (anonymously labeled) perceives the brands and the strategy. With the team together, the summary table is then presented and circulated.

When managers see these summary tables they are better able to understand why and how issues arise in relations to their branding approaches, since differing brand assumptions surface. Differences in enacting a brand strategy are recognized from the summary table. Through open discussion, the strengths and weaknesses of alternative brand interpretations are assessed and a more coherent strategy is agreed upon and implemented.

Summary

Brand management is still in its early stages though brands are a business asset. At present the tendency is still to manage products that happen to have a trade name. Yet brand management involves different and specific reasoning and approaches. The brand is not the product but it gives the product meaning and defines its identify in both time and space. Everyday branding raises new questions for managers.

Today brand management has become more of a team-based and enterprise-wide activity and sometimes it may involve as many as thirty to forty people. With senior managers striving to leverage assets across their value chain to sustain the brand's competitive advantage, there is a danger of inconsistent perceptions between team members. Brand taxonomies reveal the nature of a brand and the most appropriate strategies. By getting individual managers to categorize their brand and the strategy they are exhorting their departmental colleagues to follow, diversity between team members is identified and through greater consultation result in a more coherent approach. Having resolved internal issues about the nature of the brand, the brand's team is well prepared to move ahead to deal with other tactical issues through different component parts: the brand name, the logo, packaging, advertising, promotion and interactivity.

CHAPTER 9

Branding for Success

Although you can still hear people say "the logo is the brand" or "the company name is the brand" this is not so. A name or logo is meaningless if it does not communicate a brand's covenant with the consumer. Some of the unusual names that companies recently adapted are not really much different from the kind of product names that pharmaceutical or automobile companies gave their products over the last ten years.

While some names are pulled out of thin air, many have been the results of consideration. For example, Altria is the new name that Philip Morris, the tobacco and food company, has chosen for itself. The name is derived from the Latin word "altus," meaning to "reach higher". Verizon, created by the merger of Bell Atlantic and GTE, is a telecommunications giant. The name Verizon combines the Latin word "veritas", meaning truth, with the word horizon. The company says its "veritas values' include integrity and respect, while its "horizon values" include imagination and passion. There is no brand without a name or a logo or some sort of associated images, but branding is a deceptively simple concept. The success of a name brand or trademark is largely a function of the successful design and implementation of the branding strategy. Even today there is no single complete definition of a "brand". Some common definitions include:

A name, sign or graphic symbol or figure used to identify items or services of the seller and to differentiate them from competition.

A brand is a collection of perceptions in the mind of the consumer.

A brand is a "mental box" that reflects a set of assets (or liabilities) linked to a brand's name and symbol that adds to the value provided by a product or service…" (David Aaker).

A brand is a promise. By identifying and authenticating a product or service it delivers a pledge of satisfaction and quality (Walter Landor).

Branding is in fact a strategic point of view and a key linkage between the company's corporate goal and all its marketing activities, not a select set of activities.

Branding is central to creating customer value, not just images, store or packaging design and customer service guidelines.

Branding strategies must not only carefully "engineered" into the overall marketing mix but also into the overall customer service process re-design.

Branding should not be confused with "corporate identity" or "corporate image". The brand is not simply a reflection of a mission statement made in vacuum; it establishes the direction, leadership, clarity of purpose, inspiration and energy. It conveys the essence, character and purpose of a company and its products and services.

Communication of a product's physical attributes and functional benefits is straightforward and fast, communication of brand values is inherently circuitous and slow. Like the character of an individual, the character of a brand is most difficult to impart proactively.

The individual does not declare his character; the observer must decipher it, an indirect process that requires time and consistency. Contrary to product communication, which is best based on one single-minded forceful proposition, brand character, like the character of a person, becomes better defined as it gains in complexity.

While the product manager needs superior knowledge of his consumer to be effective, the brand manager's success depends upon his knowledge of the idiosyncrasies and values professed by the company and its long-term corporate players (top management).

Although a myriad of books and research have been published on the subject of brands and branding, we are not much closer to a clear understanding. An excellent contribution from Professor David Aaker brings some clarity. However, the panoply of buzzwords for talking about branding do more harm than good. Often brand is used to solve problems that are not brand problems. Only recently top strategy consulting firms started to approach branding as a specialized business practice. Creativity has always dominated the development of brand.

Many brand concepts basically draw upon a broad cultural legacy. Look at the history of religious imagery; consider some of the greatest religions of the world; Roman Catholicism, Islam and Buddhism etc. They all use architecture, art, symbols, music and ceremony to create unique positioning and experience.

The efforts of ancient rulers and monarchies to stamp their monumental identifications on cultural landscapes are other examples of early brand building. These landmarks, change and shape our collective response to brands. Many of them are active agents of meaning. Unlike mere words, these icons transcend the mediating and representation as forms of language. For some, these symbols echo beliefs more deeply and evoke meaning without the intermediation of any rational understanding or logic. A religious icon and its meaning fuse into a singular moment of truth to the deepest levels of the human psyche.

When a king or queen pledges to protect the lands of his people from invaders his coat of arms symbolizes the rule of law, peace and justice. It is the reminder of a social contract between the ruler and his people. The common attributes of what we might call brand equities are: a promise, relationship, standard; and common good. They are not much different from key elements of any successful brand: a brand promise, a transactional relationship, a standard for quality, and common values.

Brand management has taken place for years without theory. Today, however, there are fundamental questions about brand management's underlying principles. Many still equate great advertising to successful brand building. Yet advertising lacks consistently dynamic effects because of competition. The romanticized view of advertising is that it can always change what people think about your brand. *However, the realistic view is that advertising does not change what people think about your brand which is always hard, but only to cause them think about your brand.* A focus group subject once famously said, as recounted by Jeremy Bullmore, the former chairman of J. Walter Thompson, " I know all these brands are the same, I just have to decide which is best."

Although "common sense" this is currently practiced, there are in fact four different approaches that inherently guide branding. They are: Branding by Planning; Branding by Imageries; Branding by Experience and Branding by Self-Expression.

- **Branding by Planning**: Branding here is approached as part of a formal strategic planning process. Most of the time this occurs in the context of strategic marketing planning. The typical approach uses portfolio and product life cycle

171

concepts together with overall market overviews and competitive intelligence. The information is distilled and analyzed through each individual brand's past performance in terms of market share and margin contribution. The heart of the exercise is positioning to ensure that products cover all necessary profitable or emerging segments and use brand to achieve these objectives.

- **Branding by Imageries**: This is approached in a more functional manner. Usually advertising agencies take a leading role and advertising is linked to branding. The levers of brand building consist mainly of TV commercials, big posters and print advertisements etc. In some cases, a first showing of a 60 second TV spot during the Super Bowl is a milestone of the brand building effort. Agencies closely link the brand to advertising execution. The risk here is advertising failure means brand failure. However, a great campaign produces a very desirable brand.

- **Branding by Customer Experience**: This involves a large service component in the product offering as well within the brand promise. The customer becomes the most important part of the brand. Over the years many brands have transformed themselves into experience brands by creating a compelling customer experience. Starbucks and Body Shop did not use mass advertising to build brands. Instead, they put their resources into designing and delivering unique experiences. The Tiffany experience consists of not only the purchase experience, but also the whole experience of giving and receiving something special. The Tiffany trademark experience is inseparably linked to the ageless elegance and quality that define the brand. The blue box serves as an identifier and sensory reminder.

- **Branding by Self-Expression**: These companies put the role of brand building into the hands of customers. This has long been practiced by industries such as the fashion industry, where there's never enough time to build a relevant and meaningful a brand that keeps pace with fast-changing customer needs. Consumers also do not want to use the brand to endorse or reflect his or her personality; rather it contributes to building a personal or individual brand. In another words, strong brand identities deter customers because they dominate. The brand only requires some associated meaning so customers can mix and match with other values he or her identifies with as part of building his or her "Me" brand.

Figure 9-1 Branding Taxonomies

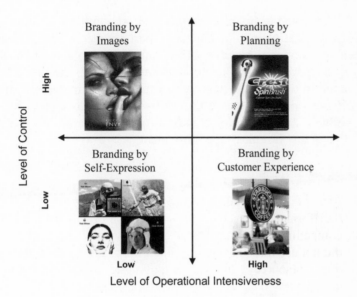

Level of Operational Intensiveness

Brand takes time to build, but what is new is the swift emergence of young brands that—in a marketing environment marked by media fragmentation, changing technology, and demanding customer—are capturing brand strength for greater than long-standing incumbent brands. The strength of such brands is matched only by the speed at which they are being built.

Many once strong corporate brands have suddenly decided it is now time to re-brand. During the past 10 years, 39 of the top 50 Fortune 500 brands dropped from the list. Building a brand once took decades. Now it is done in a few years. An example is 15-year old Starbucks, whose brand strength is greater than 108-year old Maxwell

House. Starbucks has more brand power than Folgers or Maxwell House.

Older brands like Campbell Soup and AT&T still have great strength, but relative newcomers as diverse as Virgin Airlines, Victoria's Secret, eBay, Yahoo, Amazon.com, Microsoft, Starbucks and Charles Schwab have reached the same levels of strength with remarkable speed.

These young brands generate their strength by creating and consistently delivering distinctive performance benefits and compelling emotional benefits which infuse the brand's personality with market power. These new brands are shortening the lifecycle of their brand propositions. Research reveals that an average retail lifecycle fell from 12 years in the 1970s to less than 4 years by the early 2000s. As a result, brands evolve constantly to remain distinctive in this fast moving environment.

Figure 9-2 Brand Strengths

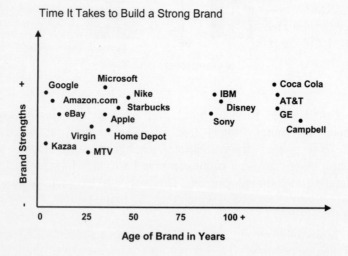

The old rules of branding do not necessarily apply—when customer needs, marketing methods, media and technology change rapidly. Strong brands succeed because they understand the new rules of branding and play by them. Knowing the new rules can help both newcomers and incumbents build and revitalize their brands—and do so at a much faster speed than ever before. Organizations need to adopt new approaches to ensure that their brands continue to stay relevant.

Three Dimensional Branding

Strong imageries, a central, core functional benefit and a strong brand personality distinguish the brand. Brand is often highlighted in multi-million dollar TV and promotional campaigns, but is easily isolated.

Three-dimensional branding goes beyond the core benefit and adds an experiential dimension to power the brand engine. Products are not merely positioned with a functional approach, stressing product features and quality, with little room to differentiate the brands. The latter gives brand a "me-too" status, which, in today's crowded marketing environment, simply makes them vulnerable to attack.

Figure 9-3 Branding Relationship and Customer Touch Points

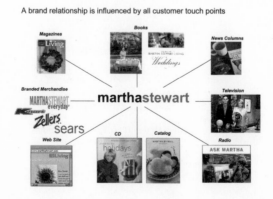

175

Creating a brand "relationship" and "experience" entails clearly defining your brand identity and customer value proposition to drive and align every customer touch point. The goal is to ensure that every customer 's brand experience is coherent, accessible—and most of important - highly satisfying.

The "three-dimensional" approach creates opportunities for experience and relationship differentiation. Smart brand builders use these emerging opportunities to increase performance distinction and enhance their brand's personality.

Saturn's brand position, for example, has influenced the way its target customers think about buying mid-priced cars. Saturn customers highly value a friendly, "no-haggle" shopping experience that includes the ability to choose options and apply for financing over the internet. Owners' clubs and events are an innovative effort to further involve the customer in the after-sale experience.

Figure 9-4 Brand-Customer Relationship Framework

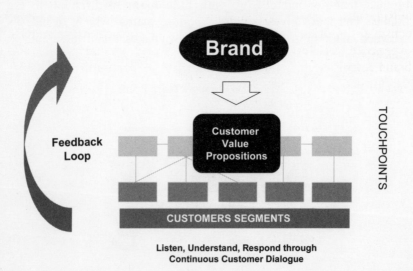

Ultimately, brand personality is intertwined with the "hard" elements of the proposition. Providing strong emotional benefits and bringing the brand to life for the customer remain as critical as ever. Fortunately, process and relationship needs create even more opportunities for brand personality. By linking corporate aspirations and brand experience, you can make the leap to a brand position and essence that defines the brand for your company's customers and employees.

For example, Starbucks Coffee created performance distinctiveness by serving its selection of coffee (functional benefit), hiring and training high-quality frontline "baristas" to provide superior in-store service, and creating an inviting retail atmosphere. All are "hard" benefits. Then, by understanding consumers' emotional needs, Starbucks brought these performance dimensions to life by positioning itself as a place where customers find a relaxed retreat and affordable escape from their hectic lives at work and at home. This develops a strong link between the brand strategy and brand experience.

What's an experience? A corporation has values that the outsider discovers bit by bit. This unveiling occurs slowly, as the consumer, a keen observer, builds his/her image of a brand's experience based on the subtle signs, brief contacts during which the brand reveals itself incidentally and often unintentionally. At times, the brand may have special opportunities, character-defining moments, which allow it to unveil more about its values and further its definition.

This is what happened when Johnson & Johnson reacted to the Tylenol tampering scare by immediately withdrawing its product from the shelves and innovating the concept of sealing its containers. By doing so, it took advantage of a rare "experience-defining moment" and sent the world a message about some of its values. The message, though subtle, was "our customers count more than protecting profits". This had positive effects not only on the corporation but also on the Tylenol brand, which, emerged from the ordeal stronger than ever.

While the values of a corporation eventually make their way through the brand's communication to the consumer's mind, there are many different factors that slow down or interrupt the process. Management changes, company mergers or acquisitions, changes in advertising agency, short-term tactical pressures are some such factors.

Any behavior or message that is out of character, during that period when the consumer determines brand character, brings the definition process back to step one. It is therefore important for the corporation to create a document that reflects what the intended brand character is, and create systems to ensure it is respected and complied with.

Figure 9-5 Branding Values

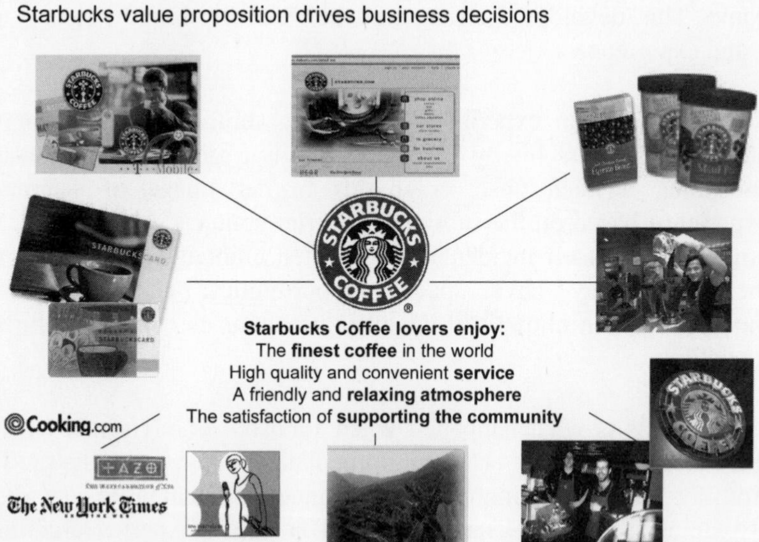
Starbucks value proposition drives business decisions
STARBUCKS COFFEE
Starbucks Coffee lovers enjoy:
The finest coffee in the world
High quality and convenient service
A friendly and relaxing atmosphere
The satisfaction of supporting the community
Cooking.com
TAZO
The New York Times

Marketing, which orchestrates only a small part of the brand experience, puts the face on the brand and makes a set of promises. Traditional organizational design, systems and structures prevent the creation of a relevant, holistic customer experience based on the brand. Although operations, sales, merchandising, inventory management, customer service, and other functions all fill an essential role in creating the customer experience, departmental goals are often disconnected from the brand. The result is not delivering upon what the brand promises, making customers feel dissatisfied and confused.

Customer experience is shaped by a series of interactions within an organization. What products or services are offered? How do they answer your request? Does the package arrive on time? Are they aware of your needs and do they take care of them? If you don't take a customer perspective when creating the customer experience, you will make it much easier for a competitor to copy your product or service and steal market share.

Figure 9-6 Branding Experience

The brand is the experience that drives the relationships

Each department in your organization should trade places with the customer and base their relationship on an outside-in perspective, creating a customer-centric experience.

Visionary companies recognize that responsibility for brand management belongs with the organization as a whole. They realize that, by aligning their organizations in a way that anticipates and fulfills their customers' emotional expectations at every customer touch point. Customer perspective shapes the brand identity, the customer value proposition and ultimately translates into a compelling and consistent customer experience, which is the starting point of a customer relationship. Every function aligns the brand with the customer perspective.

Branding Across Categories

Keeping a brand position tight and narrow within the core product segment was once the way to maintain focus and distinction. Brands are now nurtured as an asset that is profitably leveraged across product industries and segments, geographies and channels.

In the past, all copy, product, and packaging initiatives sought to reinforce a narrowly defined functional benefit for the brand in its core category. This "stick to the knitting" philosophy kept Gillette focused on razors for over 30 years and kept Duracell focused on batteries. They sought distinctiveness primarily through new functional performance. The new view is that brands develop far beyond core functional benefits, to support multiple product categories. More important, brands that are leveraged earn superior shareholder returns.

Companies with diversified brands reinforce their personalities with broad corporate image advertising on these themes. You can "do more" with American Express. IBM offers "solutions for a small planet." Though any number of companies could claim to "brings good things to life," GE has successfully claimed this phrase as its advertising slogan. Having found the golden thread and built a personality around it, diversified brands move to cross-sell and claim as their own, new industries where brand recognition is low—and where they have a competitive advantage.

American Express is a good example of cross selling. It markets a range of products and services—from financial advice to investment products and travel packages—to more than 25 million cardholders. Sears, meanwhile, successfully develops new businesses outside its core retail activities. Almost 75% of the company's growth over the past 10 years comes from non-retail sources.

During the past decade, Gillette leveraged its brand far beyond razors, into deodorants and other personal care products, with a brand promise of "the best a man can get." According to brand research, brands with this kind of aggressive leverage generate superior returns. Newer companies like Starbucks, Virgin, Sony, Calvin Klein, and Amazon.com show that leverage occurs more and more rapidly.

Of course, brands must be careful in pursuing the leverage strategy since, if not done correctly, it reduces brand distinctiveness. Given the scope and scale of a brand leverage effort, new branders have a much tighter link between their corporate and brand strategies. When brands are seen as an asset that drives growth, positioning reflects not only existing markets but also emerging opportunities. Spending on brands is truly an investment in a dynamic asset; far from being static, brands leverage into new offerings, markets, and customers.

Branding and Competitive Advantage

Branding is a potent means to establish sustainable competitive advantage. The brand culture concepts helps us see why this is the case. Brand cultures are often "sticky". Once they have been accepted as a "norm" people are usually happy to maintain the taken-for-granted understandings of the brand. There are basically two reasons for this durability.

Psychological research shows us that brand cultures are durable because people are cognitive misers. Because they are so overloaded with massive information—far more than one can reasonably digest—so they reply upon a variety of heuristics to simplify the world and their lives. Normally consumers are not interested in seeking out new information that would contradict their assumptions unless they face with a particular new problem.

Sociological research shows another reason why brand cultures are durable. Brand cultures are commonly shared by large groups of people and expressed in a number of different contexts (conversations, experiences, advertisements etc.) Brand cultures are maintained as the brand's stories, images, associations pulse through these networks. Hence, it is quite difficult for one to opt out of conventional wisdom of a brand culture and assign the brand alternative meanings.

Figure 9-7 Branding Taxonomies

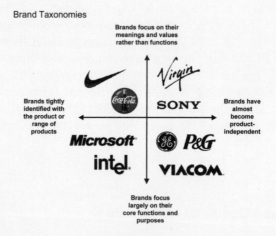

Branding Distanced from Products

Brands are often treated as products and products that have a certain level of customer awareness are treated as brands. Companies today often use the term "product manager" interchangeably with "brand manager". While most of us could think through the semantic difference between a "product" and a "brand", it seems that (with only a few exceptions) the two concepts are not distinguished when used to describe management. This is a serious mistake. The product is comprised of physical attributes, such as formulation, performance, price, ease of use, design and style. Defining a product is relatively easy. Rapid changes can be effected short term using a number of tools: just add a new ingredient or change the shape of the packaging and you have a new or, at least, a different product. A good product-marketing tactician distills a large amount of consumer, market, competition and distribution data, and boils it down to the few essential premises that form the backbone of a focused marketing plan. This forms the basis of an effective communications strategy which is based on positioning and a single-minded selling proposition known as USP (unique selling proposition).

The ability to distill facts down to this simple essence presupposes excellent knowledge and understanding of the product's buyers and consumers

The brand is almost the exact opposite. Whereas the product has form, the brand does not have a physical embodiment: it is merely a promise, a covenant with the customer. The concept of a "brand" and that of a "product" are diametrically opposed in many ways. Yet, the difference is seldom acknowledged in the way many "consumer-oriented" companies are organized: they often confuse "brand management", a strategic function, with "product management", a tactical function. The two require different skills and a different view of business. This explains why there are so many products and so few real brands.

Brands Need Parenting

One common issue today is who's in charge of the brand? Traditionally, we have asked the marketing department to define the brand, and make strategic choices as to how it is communicated within the marketplace. That department then defines the business, its vision, logistical choices and determines how the business operates, ensuring everyone that embodies the brand has complied with choices.

If there are lots of people in charge of the brand, how is activity integrated so it all looks the same from the customer's perspective? If the brand reflects the business, shouldn't the executive level be accountable for all guiding principles and alignment of the organization behind the brand? Companies need to appoint a dedicated "brand parent" with the responsibility of warding off threats to its integrity. Although you can find the title of Chief Brand Officer, it is still far from common.

Once installed, the brand parent is the mandatory gate for all brand communications, including PR, packaging, website, point-of-sale display, promotion, etc. The parent's authority is exercised worldwide. While companies spell out the authority of the global brand manager or team, they must also make the responsibilities of the country team clear. Some aspects of the brand's management are firm—the definition of what the brand stands for, for example—but others are adaptable or discretionary, such advertising or product promotions. The job of brand parent ensures that everyone knows and follows the guidelines.

Global brand teams typically consist of brand representatives from different parts of the world, stages of brand development, and competitive contexts. Functional areas such as advertising, market research, sponsorship, and promotions are also represented. The key to success with these teams is similar to those for the global brand manager.

One problem with a global brand team (unless led by a brand parent) is that no one person ultimately owns the brand globally. Thus no one is responsible for implementing global branding decisions.

In addition, team members are diverted from their task by the pressures of their primary jobs. The team lacks the authority and focus needed to ensure that recommendations are actually implemented at the country level. Mobil solves this problem in part by creating "action teams" made up of people from several countries to oversee the implementation.

Some companies partition the global brand parent or team across business units or segments. For example, Mobil has separate global brand teams for the passenger car lubricant business, the commercial lubricants business, and the fuel business because the brand is fundamentally different in each. A global brand council then coordinates those segments by reconciling the different identities and looking for ways to create brand synergy.

It is important to remember that the brand parent is not a marketing manager and does not interfere with local marketing plans that do not really affect the brand. The brand parent reports directly to the top of the corporation (president or CEO) and receives frequent public demonstrations of support from these upper echelon bosses. This helps alleviate the concerns of international managers who see the brand parent as encroaching on their own authority, or advertising agencies who see this as hindering creative freedom.

The brand parent disperses a research budget that serves to measure progress in each country towards the values of the brand in the consumer's mind. The results of this research impact compensation of local marketing staff. In addition to creating a "brand parent" function, a successful branding strategy carefully creates buy-in within an organization.

When a brand parent acts alone he or she may be perceived as another corporate staff person contributing to overhead, creating forms, and calling meetings. Adding people to the mix—in the form of a global brand team—may solve this problem. With a team working on the issue, it becomes easier to convince country brand managers of the value of global brand management.

Consider how DuPont handles its Lycra brand. The 35-year-old synthetic is known worldwide for the flexibility and comfort it lends to clothing; its identity is embodied in the global tagline "Nothing moves like Lycra."

The problem for Lycra is that it has a variety of applications —it can be used, for example, in swimsuits, in running shorts, or women's fashions. Each application requires its own brand positioning. DuPont solves the problem by delegating responsibility for each application to managers in a country where that application is strongest. Consequently, the Brazilian brand manager for Lycra is also the global brand parent for swimsuit fabric because Brazil is a hotbed for swimsuit design. Similarly, the French brand manager takes the lead for Lycra used in fashion.

The idea is to use worldwide expertise to its best advantage. The global brand parent for Lycra ensures that those in charge of different applications agree on overall strategy; he or she also pulls together their ideas in order to exploit synergies.

When local management is relatively autonomous, the brand parent or team should have a significant degree of authority. This reduces organizational or competitive pressures; in addition, it signals the company's commitment to brand building.

The team or manager may have authority over its visual representation and brand graphics, for example. In that case, the group or the individual approve any departures from the specified color, typeface, and layout of the logo. A global brand team may alternatively have authority over the look and feel of a product. The IBM ThinkPad is black and rectangular; it has a red tracking ball and a multicolored IBM logo set at 35 degrees in the lower right corner. The global brand team approves any deviations. In another example, the global brand manager at Smirnoff has sign-off authority on the selection of advertising agencies and themes.

1. Creating a Compelling Brand Story and Characters.

Experiential and relationship-based benefits add new dimensions for brands to build more exciting and relevant propositions. Forging the brand strategy starts by mapping out the consumer landscape across multiple dimensions to uncover opportunities for distinctiveness.

Consumers are analyzed by attitudinal and behavior segments and by consumption occasions; competitive shares are overlaid against those segments.

Figure 9-8 Brand Growth Acceleration.

Putting Your Brand in an Accelerated Growth Mode

Create a Compelling Brand Story	Deliver an Inspiring Brand Experience	Build Active Brand Presence	Leverage / Optimize Brand Architecture	Shift Brand Organization Development
Consumer Insight	Experience Modeling	Identify Brand Battlefields	Perform Strategic Alignment	Assign Brand Parents
Competitive Dynamics	Brand Promise Delivery	Identify Loyalty Bottlenecks	Explore and Evaluate New Products and Services Opportunities	Identify Roles and Responsibilities
Brand's Personality Dimensions	Prioritize Touch Points	Invest in Sweet Spots		Brand Performance Benchmark

The approach locates the brand's greatest strength today, as well as its greatest potential. Use customers' future rational and emotional needs to reveal process and relationship benefits that are embedded in the brand experience.

Key brand strategy questions include:

- What are your industry's key attitudinal/behavior segments and occasions?
- How much volume, profit, and growth are in each? How "movable" is the volume in the segments from competitors to your brand?
- Have you added a core set of process and relationship benefits to enhance customers' brand experience?

- What new benefits could address critical brand weaknesses, or push the strengths even higher? How are your competitors using the new dimensions to improve their brand propositions?
- How well do your 3-D performance benefits align with the brand's personality? Has the personality evolved to take advantage of the performance shifts?
- Have you linked brand strategy to your corporate strategy? How are you evolving your brand strategy to create additional opportunities for the brand?

2. Delivering an Inspiring Customer Experience.

A distinctive consumer experience that matches the brand promise requires consistency between brand promise and brand delivery. To make this happen identify and prioritize the brand's key touch points to mobilize and inspire those who deliver the brand experience. Retailers do this by creating a distinctive look and feel in the store and delivering a distinctive customer experience (Starbucks' clear guidelines to keep coffee fresh). They also hire and train evangelistic staff (leading-edge clothing retailers hiring their customers, who reinforce the brand image and model the apparel). Without such initiatives, the brand does not deliver on its promise, and brand equity is not built.

To take another example, Hertz has systematically improved its brand delivery by understanding the attributes and touch points that have the greatest impact on its desired brand position. It has identified gaps between the guidelines and actual performance, and taken initiatives to close them. Starting with the #1 Club Gold concept, Hertz has upgraded to improve brand performance (customers' names in lights, cars running upon arrival, roving check-in). It has also linked brand performance to its brand message of "Hertz Exactly," stressing how Hertz can reduce business travelers' emotional anxiety.

Frontline performance here is critical. These branders pay special attention to ensuring that employees understand the brand even better than consumers do. Starbucks, Virgin, and Home Depot all write the full stories of their brands – primarily so that their employees understand the passion and emotions of the brand.

Brands that deliver on their promises build loyalty and create high expectations and customer awareness. Failure to deliver on the promise is a fast way to permanently damage a brand. A number of banks and, most recently, electric utilities violated these principles and destroyed shareholder value.

Key brand delivery questions:

- What are the top five to seven touch points (claims for insurance, check-out for grocery, check-in/boarding for airlines) that are most critical in delivering the brand proposition?
- Have they changed over the last five years, and are they likely to change over the next five years? For each key touch point, have you translated the brand proposition into clear guidelines that align the delivery system to mobilize and inspire the people who deliver the brand experience? How well do the employees understand and deliver the desired proposition?
- What are the performance metrics for these touch points (speed and satisfaction of claims processing, speed of check-out, number of consumers surprised and delighted by the experience)? What is best practice performance? Has performance improved over time? Have the gaps versus competitors widened or narrowed over the last three years?
- Do emotional benefits reinforce the performance at the touch point? Are the brand's personality and performance benefits in harmony at the touch point? What initiatives further enliven the touch points for customers? What do brands in other industries with similar touch points teach?

3. Building Strong and Active Brand Presence

Creating superior presence requires both breadth and focus. Maximizing exposure to increase awareness (particularly for new brands) and image is a good beginning. Examples include Starbucks' use of alliances and expansion to department stores (Nordstrom), bookstores (Barnes & Noble), airlines (United Airlines), offices (IBM) and even university campuses (Harvard Business School), or Amazon.com's use of affiliate programs with thousands of smaller sites.

However, real breakthroughs in presence building come when you focus on the bottlenecks to building brand loyalty for key customer segments. Once the bottlenecks are understood, you can creatively use presence-building tools to surround consumers with the brand message. The toolkit ranges from traditional advertising to peer-to-peer and internet marketing.

Successful firms invest in the "sweet spot" of spending for each of these tools, weighing the interplay among them (understanding, for example, the impact word-of-mouth has on the effectiveness of promotions). Finally, use "brand scorecards" to monitor presence-building tools and measure the impact of spending against the company key brand's objectives.

Some key brand presence-building questions include:

- What are the critical bottlenecks for building loyalty for your brand? How do they vary by consumer segments (is the issue awareness, access, consideration, product education, or stimulating repeat usage and loyalty)?
- How creative are you in introducing new presence-building vehicles?
- How much time and resource is spent on traditional advertising and promotions versus the non-traditional options?
- How well do you understand the dynamic interplay between marketing vehicles? Do you use brand scorecards to monitor progress against your key objectives?

- Do you measure the impact of all presence-building vehicles and adjust spending accordingly?

4. Leveraging and Optimizing Brand Architecture

Deciding how to leverage a brand requires developing close ties between corporate strategy and the brand. To grow a brand into new and contiguous businesses, build a brand with a strong personality and compelling experience that drives growth, as Disney and Starbucks have done. Consumers are quite willing to allow these brands into new areas, as they have with Schwab, Virgin, and Sony. Brands that have not developed strong, cross-category performance or personality dimensions cut more easily across categories. They, however, risk diluting their core equities when they shift propositions to enter new businesses. For these brands, maintaining a focus on core performance or brand personality is key. As brands are leveraged into new situations, marketers need to consider the impact of this evolution on their overall architecture. For example, Gap uses the Gap name on BabyGap and GapKids, but went in another direction for Banana Republic and Old Navy because those brands deals with a different consumer at a different price point.

Figure 9-9 Brand leveraging Decision Map

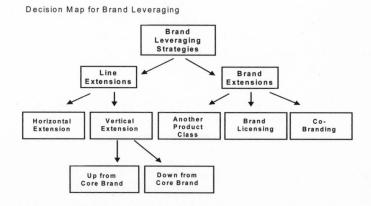

191

Key brand leverage and architecture questions include:

- What performance and personality dimensions are so strong and attached to the brand that consumers want them offered in new products or services?
- How can the brand performance and personality evolve over time to create more potential for leverage? Can the brand aspire beyond its current positioning?
- What new products and services accelerate its development?
- Are there new categories close by with relatively low "brand intensity" competitors? Are there opportunities to create a differentiated, compelling consumer offering (Sears with its extension into in-home services)?
- In target categories, does the brand offer attractive new concepts that build off strengths, while enhancing core brand?
- How do the new concepts fit into the brand architecture? Should a direct branding strategy be used, or is an indirect approach more appropriate?

5. Shifting the Brand's Organizational Development

Success with the new rules of accelerated branding requires a fundamental shift or re-organization. The organization moves from a brand management by parent approach to one based on brand management by stewardship. Working across the highest levels of a company, the brand parent (Chief Brand Officer or VP Brands) shapes the brand promises and executes, reviews, and refines the brand strategy across a multi-channel organization. This, however creates new organizational challenges:

- **Brand Parent**: Who are the brand parents? What are the brand parent's roles, responsibilities, and duties? How does the brand parent ensure the brand strategy is executed across the organization?
- **Brand Planning**: How has the brand and its touch points evolved? What actions renew distinctiveness? What are the most important opportunities for enhancing brand value?

192

What individuals or groups drive these new ventures into reality?
- **Brand Metrics**: What are the metrics for evaluation? How should the performance benchmarks be set? Who should evaluate the benchmarks, and how often?

Once marked by stability, brands have become fast-changing assets. They change to survive because customers expect more and more from them. The consumer rewards brands that deliver a strong customer experience vis a vis their expectations.

We have defined how newer brands build greater distinctiveness than incumbents. However, the new rules work just as well for established brands when they consistently deliver rich experiences at the right touch points, building explosive presence and making smart choices about brand leverage. The rules work if you want to get a real return from your brands investments. A recent McKinsey research study suggested that there is a strong relationship between the degree of a company's success in brand leverage and four key organizational elements:

- **Building brand stewardship**. Successful marketing companies view their brands as a treasured asset and treat them as such. Among the more focused brands driven CEOs such as Phil Knight at Nike, Howard Schultz at Starbucks and Mickey Drexler at the Gap are an important driving factor.
- **Embedding brand leverage**. Brand leverage is embedded in the overall strategy planning and explicitly considered at the most basic level of corporate planning. The art of branding meets the science of branding and creativity meets fact-based reality.
- **Developing supporting capabilities**. Focused brands (such as Nestlé with its brand managers) build organizations that effectively manage possible conflicts between sales channels and countries. Diversified brands (for example, Disney with its strategic planning group and Sears with its relentless focus on cross-selling) know how to develop new businesses and maximize cross-selling opportunities.

- **Putting brand metrics in place**. The least developed area of organizing for brand leverage is metrics. Emerging measures include those for the size and growth of a franchise (such as Gap's clothing consumption benchmark), or a company's share of wallet (Sears's annual survey of where consumers spend their money). Progress in building a desired image is also measured. Sharpening these metrics is increasingly important.

A big part of managing brands involves the continuous shift from brand building to brand leverage. Maintaining this balance has always been a brand management challenge. A brand only grows quickly if it maintains its performance, personality, and presence and builds on this foundation to create innovative strategies for expanding the business through focus or diversification.

Consumers enter the world of Calvin Klein via brands such as Obsession (passionate emotion), CK One (androgyny) and Eternity (idealized love). If Calvin Klein produced nothing but the occasional rehash of Obsession's "torrid sexuality" theme, the brand would not achieve the same breadth. Instead, Calvin Klein stands for strongly expressed emotion: but more than one type. Each sub-brand is a renewal, and continues to surprise the market. This heretical brand refuses to be pigeonholed.

Calvin Klein and other companies such as Martha Stewart, Nike, Sony, Disney, Coca Cola, Ralph Lauren and Starbucks are so successful in managing between brand building and brand leverage because they clearly establish which aspects of the brand are inflexible and which are subject to change. It requires a lot of planning to maintain that balance; classifying too many aspects as inflexible effectively limits the brand's extensions.

CHAPTER 10

Luxury Goods Marketing

Luxury marketing is a hot topic these days although luxury is certainly not a new concept. Luxury is as old as humanity itself. It is firmly embedded in our everyday life and collective psyche. Traditional luxury no longer exists, with few notable exceptions, such as Hermes, which remains faithful to its traditions and quality. Most luxury items today are high-end consumerism or mass-market luxury. Brands use advertising to sustain an image and appearance of luxury. It is no longer luxury, but "nouveau luxe." These items are relatively affordable, available everywhere and possess a certain glamour quotient. This is the model born in the mid-80s and that of Prada, Gucci, LVMH. They brought luxury closer to the customer, made it less difficult and therefore, less dream-like.

In the past, luxury goods typically sold in small volumes through very limited outlets to a few customers willing to pay top dollar. They formed the tip of a pyramid-shaped consumer market that got broader toward the bottom, as prices declined and distribution extended. Supported by mass marketers with big marketing war chests, mass market was king, dictating the fortunes of consumer-goods manufacturers. Today, millions of people in North America who once made up the vast middle of the continent's $8 trillion consumer market are less price-sensitive and are migrating upscale toward premium and luxury goods.

Today's auto market, for example, is increasingly "shaped like an hourglass". At the bottom, the only differentiator is price, and advantage shifts constantly between rivals that deliver the best value with the best discounts. At the top are luxury names, which rely on the cachet of their well-known brands and which are aggressively coaxing middle-class consumers to climb up the ladder. The same pattern is popping up in general and specialty retailing, consumer electronics, consumer durables and other industries, changing much conventional consumer marketing wisdom.

What's brought about this change? First, there's globalization. Thanks to free trade, the low end of the electronics market, for example, offers $59 DVD players to tempt the most price-sensitive buyers. That leaves three choices for the middle-market consumers who once would have spent a little more for a familiar brand: buy a low-end DVD player, pay more for a brand-name product with the same features, or step up to a premium brand that claims to offer higher style, quality or technology. High-end brands capitalize on this trend by making their products more attainable. Luxury-car makers, such as BMW and Mercedes-Benz, which have set sales records in recent years, spend billions on new, lower-priced models like the C-Class and A-Class to coax consumers up from the middle market.

This has pulled the rug out from under some legendary American auto brands, such as Plymouth and Oldsmobile, which once populated the broad middle but didn't have the cachet to compete with the luxury nameplates. Big luxury carmakers are also facing a big risk: They could undermine the cachet of their $70,000 top-of-the-line cars with their new sub-$30,000 offerings. And those less expensive cars may not measure up to consumers' expectations of the brand.

Towards a new definition of luxury

Luxury has not changed. What is really changing is its definition. Luxury used to be closely associated with high price, prestige and ostentation. As large segments of consumers move upscale and luxury goods move downscale, we see explosive growth in what being called the "massification of luxury goods". Massification of luxury brands has been the single most important marketing phenomenon of modern times. It goes beyond what we see today as marketers attach the notion of luxury to things that never used to be in that league. Advertising and packaging now often include words such as gourmet, premium, classic, gold and platinum. If one cannot afford to own it, now more that ever, it's possible to get a taste of these tantalizing brands if one has some patience. Thanks to eBay, more and more people have access to those out-of-reach fine things at an affordable price.

If anyone can afford luxury, then does it cease to be luxury? The answer is definitely not. It only makes these items more desirable. Social theorists are quick to emphasize the imperatives of class and identity, which they believe drives many to proclaim their superiority over others through the purchase of luxury goods.

The economic boom of the 90s created new wealth that fuelled consumption and democratized access to luxury goods. The unprecedented productivity gain in the US has allowed many to afford the previously unaffordable. As the wealthy grew richer, pressure increased on those below to trade up. As they did so, the wealthy bought and paid even more. Entered big houses, plasma TVs and the SUVs. These huge houses had to be filled with more products—great news for the home-appliance and home-furnishing industries.

197

Figure 10-2 Massification of Luxury Brands

Massification of Luxury Brands

Developed economies are wealthy. Manufacturing technological advancement, global overcapacity, the emergence of China as the world's factory and the unbeatable Wal-Mart phenomenon allow even those of lower income segments to afford luxuries such as a DVD for $40 and a complete home theatre system for $99. When individuals' physical needs are satisfied and they have everything they possibly could want or need, what's next?

That is the ultimate challenge for the luxury marketer today. Even the poorest in our society partake in luxury. Where else in the world would you find those at the bottom of the income chain owning cars, satellite TVs, big television sets, DVDs, cell phones, computers, air conditioning, and other 'luxurious' necessities of 21st century life?

The natural evolution of all luxury concepts is from class to mass. In other words, luxury is first adopted by the affluent and wealthy. Then inevitably it is translated and reinterpreted down to the mass market. Today's luxuries become tomorrow's necessities. As luxury marketers, we have to stay out in front of luxury consumers, discovering new and different ways to give expression to the their desires. New technology creates new luxury needs and business opportunities, such as plasma televisions, enhanced PDA's and digital photography equipment. Changes in fashion, too, are a way to continually reinvent luxury; so today colored diamonds are hot. Yet, to assure the greatest long-term success, luxury marketers need to connect with the luxury consumers' inner emotional lives and create new products and services to meet those needs.

The imbalance in our current spending patterns may perhaps be viewed as a market failure caused by consumption externalities: greater consumption by one group of people actually imposes costs on others. An important strategic advantage of this explanation is that it is grounded in the very same theoretical framework that animates the beliefs of the most ardent defenders of the status quo. Thus, as even conservative economists have long recognized, when one family's spending decisions impose negative consequences on others, Adam Smith's invisible hand simply cannot be expected to produce the best overall spending pattern.

The good news is that if consumption externalities are what lead us to work harder, thereby improve productivity, spend more and it boosts our consumer-driven economy, although consumers save little and help the explosive growth of credit card and personal finance companies.

Watch out for a new brand of consumer in 2005: the middle-aged ex-yuppies who, surrounded by too much stuff acquired over the years, decide to simplify life. Luxury purchases, conspicuous consumption and a trophy culture may be discarded in pursuit of a more relaxed and uncluttered lifestyle. These experienced luxury spenders will buy more ephemeral, less tangible stuff: fleeting, but expensive, experiences, not heavy goods for the home.

Another new brand of consumer is typified by the character Carrie Bradshaw in the TV series "Sex and the City". Just like Carrie, who has more than a hundred pair of shoes but cannot get a mortgage because she has no savings in the bank or financial assets of any kind. A new kind of luxury consumer is "taste-rich but cash-poor". These individuals (who wear $30 tops from J.Crew with $2,000 Hermes

Birkin handbags and have a collection of Manolo Blahnik shoes) are well educated and extremely knowledgeable about what they're buying and they are most demanding, show little brand loyalty and are obsessively materialistic.

During the economic boom of the 90's the new wealth's obsession with status and designer labels meant Prada, Dior, Kate Spade, Hermes, Gucci, Burberry and Louis Vuitton could sell loads of items without having to do much marketing other than spectacular fashion shows and advertising in fashion magazines.

It is easy to develop lazy habits such as not giving people a reason other than status to buy their goods. "It didn't matter to them if you actually appreciated the taste or style of the product," says Kim Faulkner, a managing director of US consultants Interbrand. So people did things like pour water or soft drinks into expensive champagne bottles. For today, if a company to effectively target different luxury markets, they need a strong vision and an innovative business model to capture new opportunities.

Luxury consumers expess self-actualization needs

Luxury consumers express self-actualization needs as they turn from a pursuit of materialism to a yearning for new experiences. My research in the luxury market shows that when consumers buy luxury things, they are attempting to achieve a feeling or to enhance an experience. Luxury product marketers need to study how the products they sell further an emotional experience for the consumer and the product help the user to construct a self-identity. This, then, becomes the focus of luxury marketing, giving new meaning to the phrase "experiential marketing."

Experience marketing infuses all product development, marketing and sales efforts with the *feeling* that the product promises to convey to the customer. Rather than stressing product features or up-scale brand image in advertising, (such as the exquisite craftsmanship and finest quality materials,) advertising communicates

200

the emotion that the product inspire in consumers. Luxury goods need to be sold, advertised and marketed differently.

Luxury consumers express desire beyond prestige

- "You reach a point where you don't want stuff anymore. Over the years you accumulate stuff and once you have everything you want, you come to the point where it is enough. There are other important things in life, like relationships, experiences and spirituality."
- "It's changed over time. When we were first married, I appreciated products, but now I seek services. We learn to appreciate the experiences more because those are things that nobody can ever take from you. Personal things that we are doing for ourselves are important."
- "After you've reached your fifties, you avoid 'stuff.' You just want quality rather than quantity. Not only the traditional sense of quality and workmanship, but also something that makes it special. "
- "During my life, we had varying amounts of income. But even before we had a large income, different things would have been considered a luxury to me. But now those things that I used to consider luxuries have changed. Yet I still cherish some of them."
- "When you are free from the children and those expenses you have more expendable income. I love to travel and play golf. I never had an opportunity to do that when I was raising a family. Our money went toward necessities, but now we can spend it on more luxuries."
- "The first half of my life is ruined by our parents and the second half by our children. I don't mind spending on things that we really deserve."
- "You ask yourself how many more years you have when you hear about people who are sick. I say, 'Seize the day.' If I want something, I will buy it as long as I have the means. Even if sometimes I don't."

There is a different tenor to luxury marketing today. What you buy is more important than what you earn. Luxury is not a goal anymore. For many, it has become a necessity. Although the purchases are the same, motivations are different. While consumers are always eager to rationalize their luxury purchases, today they do so based on a different value system. Today's luxury drivers are rooted much more firmly in personal well-being and self-satisfaction while purchases such as jewelry, watches and handbags continue to satisfy the desire and to indulge one-self and one's loved ones.

Below, further insights into luxury goods purchase behavior:

- **Real vs. Imaginary**- Consumption sometimes operates at a level of the imaginary, but it also has real effects in facilitating the construction of self-identity. While luxury shoppers are led by rational desire to purchase items of high value and craftermanship, eight of the ten top purchase motivators are emotionally driven. Marketers must tap into consumers' desires for well-being, self-concept and indulgence. The consumption of symbolic meaning, reinforced through advertising, provides the individual with the opportunity to construct, maintain and communicate identity and social meanings. Victoria Secrets is a great example of a marketer using the unobtainable, imaginary dreams of its consumers to drive sales. Beautiful and perfectly proportioned models strut down the runway and grace glitzy catalog pages to convey the notion that the company's products can enhance—or even instill such glamour. If Victoria's Secret products are worn by the beautiful, does the inverse also hold true? Will wearing them make one beautiful? Women scoop up the product for themselves and dazzling elegance will rub off the wearer. Ask this important question: What are your key target segments' wildest imaginations?
- **Material vs. the Symbolic** After a product fulfills its ability to satisfy a physical need, we enter the realm of the symbolic, and it is symbolic meaning that is used in the search for the meaning of existence. We become consumers of "illusions". De Beers' slogan "A diamond is forever" has been so

successful in creating the illusion of "love and eternity" that a diamond is the material symbol of love and marriage. For many, the gift of a diamond symbolizes eternal love, which in itself is an elusive concept. Now marketers are trying to do the same with platinum. Ask this important question: What illusions does your product help consumers to create or maintain?

- **Social vs. the Self** - The function of symbolic meanings of products operate in two directions, outward in constructing the social world—social-symbolism—and inward towards constructing our self-identity: self-symbolism. In other words, using products to help us become our "Possible Selves". Most SUVs and sports equipment brand images are built on this very concept. SUVs have an image of being sporty, powerful, tough and rugged. They appeal to men (and some women) who may not travel anywhere more treacherous than the local supermarket. The Hummer sold to civilians is radically different from the one used by the military, yet the brand's image, as an enduring, robust all-terrain vehicle remains intact. Expensive and "cool", SUVs are popular yet practical—they hold a carpool full of kids and their hockey equipment—without saddling their upscale owners with an "minivan" image. Ask this important question: What are your target luxury segments' ideal possible selves?

- **Desire vs. Satisfaction** - Advertising often provides gratification and recodes a commodity as a desirable psycho-ideological ideal. In fact, it feeds the desire to achieve the often unobtainable unity of the self, using destabilized meanings and images that separate products from their original intended use and offer the opportunity to reconstruct a self by purchasing meanings in a do-it-yourself fashion. Desire exists in the gap between visual / languages and the unconscious. Desire does not want satisfaction. To the contrary desire desires desire. Images are often so appealing that things cannot satisfy. Humans have a natural ability to want, desire, aspire, yearn, and long for. Any attempt to diminish this natural desire is counterproductive, frustrating, and improbable. Some people desire desirelessness with such a passion that it actually increases their ability to desire. What we do we become stronger in, and these people yearn so much and so often to have no more yearning that their ability to yearn becomes astronomical. Postmodern consumption is inextricably linked with aspects of sexuality, both conscious and subconscious. Desires are constructed through linkages between consumption and the human body. Visuals continue to be the most powerful tool because they never satisfy. Calvin Klein, Gucci and Abercrombie and Fitch built and maintain their brands based entirely on this concept. Meaning is created through a continuous search for links between identity (social) and the self. Ask this important question: What are the unobtainables that your brands are based on?

Summary

Marketing of luxury goods is in the middle of a transformation. The individual must experience consumption as part of the journey towards personal development, achievement and self-creation. They are content to map their lives on a marketer's segmentation chart. Marketing of luxury goods is evolving away from a top-down approach towards one that provides or facilitates innovations for new ideas and meanings. The co-creation of brand meanings with consumers has become the basis for value. This, in fact, challenges the convention view of product-centric innovation.

The success of marketing relies heavily on its ability to co-develop and embed meanings in brands and products. This leads to the important conclusion that meaning does not necessary emanate from the material or functional aspects of products or services. Consumer understandings and experiences of what are seemingly objective properties are simply "culturally constructions". Brands have symbolic meanings in all cultures and societies. Marketers need to induce the consumer with a preference to pay a premium for products that are basically more mass-produced similar quality products.

CHAPTER 10

Organizing for Marketing Excellence

When Regis McKenna - the patriarch of modern marketing—talks about "the death of marketing", he's referring to marketing becoming an integrated part of any organization, rather than just a specific function. Brand managers, marketing planners and advertising managers always dominated marketing. Now, marketing capabilities are becoming critically essential for all companies who compete for market leadership.

To deliver superior performance and create competitive advantage, companies need a new breed of marketers who bring a new set of skills and competencies. We have often read stories about companies made huge marketing and customer relationship management investments, yet failed to improve marketing or build customer relationships.

They hired top brand executives, launched big advertising campaigns, spent millions creating flashy websites and poured many millions into CRM systems. Many of them installed CRM systems and thought the work done. CRM requires constant tinkering and experimentation and most companies simply cannot afford this on a systematic basis. The goal is to have a CRM system that makes customers feel the overall customer experience is better than that of competitors. As many companies become aware of this, installing CRM systems becomes something of an arms race. The technology is diffusing pretty rapidly and many get stuck in the Red Queen syndrome—you run faster and faster just to stay in place.

So the question is if CRM is definitely not the answer, how can companies transform themselves into top marketers and what core competencies or distinct capabilities are required? The answer is there are no silver bullets or magical software application packages that all companies can use. However, there are a number of actions you can take to make real improvements. Six important steps that help companies drive marketing performance follow. These six steps are relevant, practical guidelines for any CEO who wants his company's marketing performance to grow to the next level:

1. Start with a well articulated corporate strategy and clearly defined set of company marketing performance objectives

The goal is not simply to improve marketing capabilities but rather to achieve bottom line results. Goals include both realistic tangible targets and intangible objectives that form the basis of a clearly articulated marketing strategy that values, accesses, serves and retains customers.

In personal financial services, a medium size bank set the goal of doubling the company's growth rate. In order to meet this challenge, the business unit invested heavily in developing superior capabilities in product management, marketing and sales. Marketing skill building was critical to the success of an airline that recognized it needed to build customer loyalty to protect its market share in light of more of aggressive competition. Similarly, several retail chains improved their capabilities to attract younger customers with different needs and shopping preferences to replace a dwindling base of aging customers.

Driving marketing improvement efforts with performance goals is key because it forces management to acknowledge the marketing challenge and gaps. Recognition of a specific marketing need to generate revenue, increase customer loyalty and grow a particular segment creates practical business platforms that everyone understands and supports. Most important, the focus of performance establishes a clear way to measure and communicate marketing impact and ensures a clear sense of purpose.

This performance orientation also silences the critics who often fail to recognize the tangible importance of marketing to companies' shareholder value. A recent example would be Motorola. After some market setbacks it launched a range of new products and initiated an image building advertising campaign to boost its anemic brand image. It ranked 66th in the 2000 survey of the world's most powerful brands by Interbrand, a marketing and brand consulting firm. Motorola's competitors such as Nokia was ranked 5th and Ericsson, 36th. After hiring a top-notch marketer from athletic shoe giant Nike Inc., Motorola has a goal of making itself a top-ten brand within 3 years.

2. Achieve leadership in your industry in at least one core marketing skill important to your business

After all major marketing performance goals and metrics are set, it's time to choose what to build and just as important, what not to. Determine what to outsource and what to maintain at an industry level. The objective to become a world-class marketer is far too broad. Marketing involves many skills sets. It is literally impossible for any company to excel in all of them.

For example, just think of the different people and training required, level of investment needed, to excel in mass advertising and brand building versus technology-intensive, relationship-based and experience-driven marketing. While many of today's companies use most of these marketing tools, not many of them have distinct competencies in several. The success of American Express in the eighties is due to their distinct capabilities in database-driven direct marketing. Amway's success is attributed to their distinct capabilities in community-based multi-level marketing. The reality is that no company can afford to build many skills and will not be able to lead in more than one. The key is to understand the strategic market levers and put resources and energy behind them.

All successful companies clearly understand the one or two marketing capabilities that put them in front for competitive advantages. For example, marketers such as Louis Vuitton focus on managing and maintaining brand image. Its highly exclusive distribution network is key to superior business performance. Nike's focus on image-based advertising and college sponsorship are factors in their long-term success. For United Airlines, their decision to focus on building a sophisticated tactical pricing system for yield management was crucial to bottom line performance in the tough airline business. As the marketing landscape changes and new skills continue to emerge, making the right choice is tougher. The proliferation of customer data and emerging marketing technologies add to the challenge causing companies to struggle with whether to invest in industry specific customer management systems or advanced predictive modeling to enable effective cross selling.

Marketers used to have a broad set of skills; today they are becoming specialized. A common complaint among CEOs is that packaged goods marketers are not adept at driving database-marketing programs. On the other hand, database-marketing experts often lack segmentation and communications skills. Marketing is such a broad field, matching marketers' skill sets with company needs adds another dimension to an already complex choice. With this in mind, diagnose what specific areas are crucial to supporting your business strategy. Then find and close that gap.

For example, if a company finds that its customer retention, email marketing and customer service capability are critical yet underdeveloped, skill building in these areas become priority. Galvanizing resources and energy to build one or two of the three targeted marketing skills that yield the highest and immediate return is the goal. Average marketing skills, even if broadly based are almost a proven formula to lag behind the market leaders. You must align your marketing capability building to your overall business strategy and value creation process. Some capabilities cannot be built in-house then out-sourcing needs to be considered.

3. Understand the basis of customer relationships and manage them effectively across all touch points

"Everybody is scrambling to integrate all their customer contact points. At this early stage, much of the effort has gone into computers and related equipment, though many companies adopting the technology aren't yet clear about what their systems will really have to do to build enduring and profitable relationships with customers", says George Day, a professor at Wharton. In fact, much of the argument surrounding CRM centers on the technology, diverting attention from the more critical issue: What is the "basis" of customer relationships and how can customer strategies be most effectively crafted to manage them? This precedes functionality and technical architecture. Effective CRM technologies exist, but they produce true value only when properly deployed in support of winning customer strategies.

So what constitutes a relationship? While companies often use this word casually, customers are protective of the word "relationship." They do not use it indiscriminately. When asked to talk about their relationships, regardless of context, they talk about family, friends and neighbors. They might next extend the word to business associates, doctors and personal trainers. While many consumers uses the word "relationship" within a business context they do so when referring to people they have been doing business with for some time.

Evidence suggests that while consumers do acknowledge the existence of relationships with commercial entities, they divide them into three basic categories. Their level of loyalty, trust and expectations varies between these categories. Not all business relationships are positive ones. As in our personal lives, there are some interactions or relationships that we are forced into or have little choice about.

The top category consists of firms the consumer has dealt with for a long time, engendering trust. Generally, a personal (face to face) relationship with a representative of the company exists. Expectations are high and delivery on "the promise" presumed.

The second category is comprised of companies that provide satisfactory services at competitive prices, perhaps in a convenient manner. The product usually does not require high consumer involvement. Expectations are moderate, as is consumer loyalty. Consequently, barrier to exit programs are often used as a customer retention tool.

The final category consists of businesses with whom the customer conducts an impersonal transaction. The offerings usually require low involvement and service in the industry is similar among competitors. Can a business selling groceries (for example) claim a relationship with its customers? Consumers must buy groceries, but not necessarily from a particular business. Loyalty based on habit or inertia is of dubious value, since the reasons for continued patronage are not positive. Many customers seek low prices, good service, and convenience: if you deliver these you have a better chance of engendering loyalty in your customers than by running a comprehensive CRM system.

The nature of company offerings, customer value propositions, segmentation strategy and the nature of competition must be analyzed in order to understand the "basis" of the relationship, the starting point of any CRM strategy. Relationship marketing always presents considerable barriers particularly in consumer markets. The size of these markets, the lack of consumer interest in a "real" relationship, and the persistence of aggressive advertising and sales promotion-driven strategies all create challenges. Some challenges are met through CRM technology, but companies with millions of customers always have different (weaker) relationships with its customers than the firms with thousands of customers. Although business is growing more customer-oriented, and embracing relationship marketing, some companies "force" customers into relationships through incentives or punishments. The customer likely receives greater satisfaction from direct benefits at the point of sale.

Once relationship architecture is defined, it is applied and managed across all customers touch points. CRM technology usually plays a vital role from the perspective of revealing effective touch points and supporting service delivery, engaging customers at the right time, with the right content, on the right device. Technology investments improve consumer data and aid in touch point design and creation, execution and evaluation. To maintain the customer dialogue, every conversation element—touch point— must deliver on the actual expectations of the consumer. The goal of each touch point is to "move" a consumer along in the following two dimensions:

- First along the loyalty cycle. This is where the brand experience is created and the whole experience is built emotionally. All brands want to touch consumers' inner needs and be identified with or dreamt about.
- Second along the purchase cycle. Every touch point needs moves the consumer along the cycle from awareness, consideration and preference to purchase. A touch point that moves a consumer to order through a catalog or website, enter a promotion, or sign up to SMS alerts, makes him commit an act that reveals what drives him. Even unintended actions help construct customer profiles.

For touch points to move consumers to finish a scenario, three things must be right—context, content and channel. These must be effectively applied to the carefully designed relationship architecture. The right touch point content is the information the recipient needs to achieve one of his or her goals. Making this happen is no simple task The specific team that makes this happen includes people from all disciplines; marketing, sales, merchandising, service and technical support. Diversity ensures cross-channel consistency at all touch points.

4. Hardwire marketing into your strategic planning process

Strategic planning integrates functional processes, organizational design and goal setting. When the planning is customer-based, it forces an in-depth understanding of consumer needs, revealing the right set of marketing and business activities to outrun competitors.

Success hinges on asking the right questions and flexibility. Planning processes are subject to change and marketing objectives reinforce the links to core business processes.

One credit card company, for example, completely changed its sales planning processes to dramatically increase its customer base. It shifted its focus from annual geographical focused sales targeted at specific customer segments and developed cross-functional teams responsible for creating and implementing segment-specific plans. Incentives were linked to sub-goals for each segment. The focus of marketing activities includes:

- What did we do to gain share and why did we lose share?
- Who are our most loyal customer groups and how well are we retaining them?
- Do we really have a relationship with our core customer group? If so, what is the "basis" of that relationship?
- Who are the customer groups that we do not want and how do we avoid serving them?
- What is the level of service required to retain our core customers?

- What is the level of service required to win new customers?
- What pricing strategy and tactics best drive profit, given our understanding of customer switching patterns?
- How well do current marketing activities create awareness, maintain image, offer trials or meet objectives?
- What marketing expenditure is really required to meet objectives?
- What emerging customer needs or new marketing approaches do we test to stay ahead?
- What are the emerging technologies that drive new customer service experience and economics?

New planning processes are usually powerful performance drivers. Planning processes are redesigned to integrate business systems and facilitate understanding of the company's goals and actions across the whole organization. This provides an opportunity to learn about what is working and what is not.

With clear measures of success or failure you learn how to win the hearts and minds of customers. These measures are especially evident in initiatives that track hard data using customer analytics with near real time feedback. But other sources, such as customer feedback, surveys and front line employee feedback are also useful gauges of how well the company is doing and what needs improvement.

5. Use outsiders to drive change

Marketing is all about understanding customers' needs, meeting and communicating those needs to the right target groups in the form of compelling customer value propositions. This customer-focused mind-set sweeps across all functions in the organization. Without this, you cannot become a true market leader.

In companies known for marketing excellence (such as Nike, Starbucks, LVMH, BMW, Sony, Pepsi, P&G and Nestle) as many as one out of four of their senior managers demonstrate a customer focus daily. These include product designers, production managers and finance managers.

Sometimes you need fresh blood. Outsiders drive change in an organization. More than 75% of successful marketing companies bring professional marketers and management consultants into the company, sometimes from other industries or consulting firms. Most hired not just three or four managers but twenty to forty. More than 60% placed a significant number of people throughout the whole organization.

Companies with poor experiences in hiring outside marketers to drive change did not build critical mass. The consumer division of a media company, for example, hired one new marketing VP, then handcuffed him as he attempted to change the 70-person marketing department. This outsider failed because the entrenched incumbents vastly outnumbered and rejected the transplanted change agent.

Companies need to make tough choices in terms of people and the organization. Screen new hires not just for functional skills, but also for their ability to function and operate in the corporate culture. Make changes swiftly and decisively. Devote resources to integrate and train new and incumbent employees. The combination of new staff in critical managerial roles and marketing professionals significantly increase the marketing mindset in many companies. This talent pod provides the leadership that spurs an organization to marketing excellence.

6. Bridge the gap between CRM, marketing and Information Technology (IT) to drive return-on-relationships

Another big challenge is in the internal gap—between marketing and CRM/IT. Traditionally, marketing and IT groups do not interact strongly. IT lacks an understanding of marketing processes and users but usually has a primary influence in any CRM implementation. IT may also have limited understanding of analytical databases, having worked with general purpose IT vendors, who design systems for operational, not analytical use. This creates huge performance issues. For this reason, it is worth undertaking a comprehensive business requirements exercise before embarking on this process and infrastructure.

The world is changing, yet marketing has not caught up. The age of technology and IT has transcended from automating company processes to automating customer interaction. CRM is an increasingly critical component of the marketing mix. Yet, marketers do not usually drive this wave of activity; it is software developers and package solutions that do so.

Whole swathes of literature purport to offer the very best of CRM yet hardly mention marketing. When it does so the word seems totally interchangeable with sales. Yet, at the heart of CRM is the customer, not the process. The processes merely provide the necessary support. What the customer needs is the service/product provided on time, appropriately at a fair price. We in marketing know there is more to it than that—customers like brands and brands deliver profits. Marketing understands both customers and brands. The custodian of the customer should be marketing and not IT.

Yet as marketing technology is integrated with CRM and ERP systems responsibility for the customer relationship drifts into IT territory. The CRM puts the process before the customer. It confuses sales with marketing. CRM sells a system not a solution. The offerings of the big CRM players move quickly past customer definitions and segmentation, yet this is where CRM has to be its most precise. A company-wide definition of customers should be universally understood. How it transcends current data and knowledge is essential information. This leads to the two core reasons for disenchantment with CRM. It is important to understand the role and impact of CRM in terms of marketing from the outset. Marketing strategy does not sufficiently encompass the new CRM enabled multi-channel environment. What CRM does is provide individual customer data and the means to communicate with the consumers appropriately and cost effectively. It is a system, a process, but not a solution. The solution, as always in marketing, lies in understanding customer behavior—anticipating it, shaping it to increase profitability. That is why both marketing and brands exist.

Summary

It is inconceivable that we look in the year 2010 and will look back at the last ten years as an era of profound change—perhaps even a historic turning point. During that decade, business historians may conclude, a new bleed of market leaders emerged. These companies were not simply the younger, more vigorous offspring of the old breed; they did not just work hard to meet changing customer demands. Instead, they broke the mold and invented new marketing models and made many old breeds felt like they were trying to win the Wimbledon with a wooden tennis racquet.

Making the CEO the Chief Marketing Officer, as suggested by Regis McKenna, is still high today on many company agendas. To win customers and improve bottom line performance, they recognize the importance of building new marketing skills and capabilities in their organizations. Although each industry and each company has a different starting point and requires a different strategy, the approaches shared by companies that are successful marketing leaders are helpful models. CEOs must focus on performance goals and at least one key marketing skill to build an integrated marketing mindset. Change will not be driven by advertising agencies or outside integrated marketing consultancies, it is spurred from within the organization.

As the competitive environment grows tougher, many companies face the challenge of honing their marketing skills. By following the suggestions outlined in this book, you will be on your way to building better marketing capabilities as you strive to become a marketing leader in the decades to come.

References and further reading

Aaker, D. (1996), Building Strong Brands. The Free Press, New York, NY.

Aggarwal, P. and Cha, T. (1997), "Surrogate buyer and the new product adoption process: a conceptualization and managerial framework", Journal of Consumer Marketing, Vol. 14

Alba, J.W. and Hutchinson, J.W. (1987), "Dimensions of consumer expertise", Journal of Consumer Research, Vol. 13.

Antil, J.H. (1988), "New product or service adoption: when does it happen?", Journal of Consumer Marketing, Vol. 5.

Archilladelis, B., Schwarzkopf, A. and Cines, M. (1990), "The dynamics of technological innovation: the case of the chemical industry", Research Policy, Vol. 19.

Assael, H. (1992), Consumer Behavior and Marketing Action, PWS-Kent, Boston, MA.

Assael, H. (1992), Consumer Behavior and Marketing Action, PWS-Kent, Boston, MA.

Barczak, G.J., Bello, D.C. and Wallace, E.S. (1992), "The role of consumer shows in new product adoption", Journal of Consumer Marketing, Vol. 9.

Balmer, J.M.T. and Wilkinson, A. (1991), ``Building societies: change, strategy and corporate identity'', Journal of General Management, Vol. 17.

Balmer, J.M.T. (1995), "Corporate branding and connoisseurship", Journal of General Management, Vol. 21.

Balmer, J.M.T. (1998), "Corporate identity and the advent of corporate marketing'', Journal of Marketing Management, Vol. 14.

Barbara, V.P. and Zaltman, G. (1990). Hearing the Voice of the Market: Competitive Advantage Through Creative Use of Information. Harvard Business School Press, Boston, MA.

Benetton, L. (1994), "Franchising: how brand power works", in Stobart, P., Brand Power, Macmillan, Basingstoke.

Brady, J. and Davis, I. (1993), "Marketing's mid-life crisis", The McKinsey Quarterly, No. 2.

Brehm, J. (1956), "Post decision changes in the desirability of alternatives", Journal of Abnormal and Social Psychology, Vol. 52.

Bitner, M., Booms, B. and Mohr, L. (1994), "Critical service encounters: the employees' viewpoint'', Journal of Marketing, Vol. 58.

Boyd, W.L., Leonard, M. and White, C. (1994), "Customer preferences for financial services: an analysis", International Journal of Bank Marketing, Vol. 12.

Campbell, A. Goold, M. and Alexander, M. (1994), Corporate Level Stratey: Creating Value in Multi-Business Company. John Wiley and Sons,NY.

Cagan, J and Vogel, M. Craig. (2002) Creating Breakthrough Products: Innovation and Product Planning to Program Approval. Prentice Hall. NJ.

Christopher, M. (1996), "From brand values to customer value", Journal of Marketing Practice, Vol. 2 No. 1.

Cooper, R.G. (1993). Winning at New Products: Accelerating the Process for Idea to Launch. Addison Wesley.

Court, D., Freeling, A. and George, M. (1993), Marketer's Metamorphosis, McKinsey and Company, London.

Court, D., Forsyth., J.E., Kelly, G.C. and Loch, M.A., (2001), The New Rules of Branding, McKinsey and Company, New York.

Clayton, M. (1998), Banks should boost their brand identities'', America's Community Banker, Vol. 7 No. 12.

Clayton, M. (1997), The innovator's Dilemma, Harvard Business School Press, Boston, MA.

Day, G.S. and Schoemaker P.J.H. (2000), Wharton on Managing Emerging Technologies. John Wiley & Sons, NY.

de Chernatony, L. and McWilliam, G. (1990), "Appreciating brands as assets through using a two dimensional model", International Journal of Advertising, Vol. 9

de Chernatony, L. (1993), "Categorising brands", Journal of Marketing Management, Vol. 9.

de Chernatony, L. (1996), "Brand Taxonomies", Marketing Intelligence and Planning Vol. 14.

de Chernatony, L. and McDonald, M.H.B. (1992), Creating Powerful Brands, Butterworth-Heinemann, Oxford.

DMB&B (1994), A New Strategy for Leadership, DMB&B, London.

Dowling, G.R. and Staelin, R. (1994), "A model of perceived risk and intended risk-handling activity", Journal of Consumer Research, Vol. 21.

Dolan, J. and Hermann S. (1996) Power Pricing: How Managing Price Transforms the Bottom Line. The Free Press, New York, NY.

Doyle, P., (1995), "Marketing in the new millennium", European Journal of Marketing, Vol. 29.

Fisher, R.J. and Price, L.L. (1992), "An investigation into the social context of early adoption behavior", Journal of Consumer Behavior, Vol. 19.

Fiske, S.T, (1982), "Social cognition and affect", in Harvey, J. (Ed.), Cognition, Social Behavior, and the Environment, Hillsdale, NJ.

George, M., Freeling, A. and Court, D. (1994), "Reinventing the marketing organization", The McKinsey Quarterly, Vol. 4

Glaister, K. and Thwaites, D. (1993), "Managerial perception and organizational strategy", Journal of General Management, Vol. 18.

Grewal, D., Gotlieb, J. and Marmostein, H. (1994), "The moderating effects of message framing and source credibility on the price-perceived risk relationship", Journal of Consumer Research, Vol. 21.

Guadagni, P.M. and Little, J.D.C. (1983), ``A logit model of brand choice calibrated on scanner data", Marketing Science, Vol. 2.

Gupta, A.K. and Rogers, E.M. (1991), "Internal marketing: integrating R&D and marketing within the organization", Journal of Consumer Marketing, Vol. 8.

Hammer, M. and Champy, J. (1993), Re-engineering the Corporation, Harper Collins, London.

Hamel, G. and Prahalad, C. (1994), Competing for the Future, Harvard Business School Press, Boston, MA.

Herbig, P.A. and Kramer, H. (1994), "The effect of information overload on the innovation choice process: innovation overload", Journal of Consumer Marketing, Vol. 11.

Hooley, G.J. and Saunders, J. (1993), Competitive Positioning: The Key to Market Success, Prentice-Hall, Hemel Hempstead.

Iacobucci D. (2001). Kellogg on Marketing. John Wiley and Sons, NY.

Jones, J.M. and Ritz, C.J. (1991), "Incorporating distribution into new product diffusion models", International Journal of Research in Marketing, Vol. 8.

Jolly, K. Vijay. (1997), Commercializing New Technologies: Getting From Mind to Market. Harvard Business School Press, Boston, MA.

Kapferer, Jean-Noel. (2001) Reinventing The Brand. Kogan Page. CT.

Kalwani, M.U., Yim, C.K., Rinne, H.J. and Sugita, Y. (1990), ``A price expectations model of consumer brand choice'', Journal of Marketing Research, Vol. 27, August.

Katsanis, L.P. and Pitta, D.A. (1995), "Punctuated equilibrium and the evolution of the product manager", Journal of Product and Brand Management, Vol. 4.

Keller, K.L. (1993), "Conceptualizing measuring and managing customer-based brand equity", Journal of Marketing, Vol. 57.

Kotler, P. and Armstrong, G. (1996), Principles of Marketing, 7th ed., Prentice-Hall, Englewood Cliffs, NJ.

Kotler, P. (1999), Kotler on Marketing. The Free Press, New York, NY.

Kotler, P. (1980), Marketing Management: Analysis, Planning and Control, Prentice Hall, Englewood Cliffs, NJ.

Kiesler, S. and Sproull, L. (1982), "Managerial responses to changing environments", Administrative Science Quarterly, Vol. 27.

Kuchinskas, S. (2000) "The End of Marketing", Business 2.0, November.

Lee, M. and Na, D. (1994), "Determinants of technical success in product development when innovative radicalness is considered", Journal of Product Innovation Management, Vol. 11.

Levitt, T. (1980) "Marketing Success Through Differentiation of Anything". Havard Business Review.

Levitt, T. (1974) "Marketing Myopia". Harvard Business Review.

Lifton, D.E. and Lifton, L.R. (1989), "Applying the Japanese 'thin market' strategy to industrial new product development", International Journal of Technological Management, Vol. 4.

Lunsford, D.A. and Burnett, M.S. (1992), "Marketing product innovations to the elderly: understanding the barriers to adoption", Journal of Consumer Marketing, Vol. 9.

Larson, J. and Christensen, C. (1993), "Groups as problem solving units", British Journal of Social Psychology, Vol. 32.

Malhotra, N.K. (1982), "Information load and consumer decision making", Journal of Consumer Research, Vol. 8

Meyers-Levy, J. and Tybout, A.M. (1989), "Schema congruity as a basis for product evaluation", Journal of Consumer Research, Vol. 16.

Mintzberg, H. and Waters, J. (1982), "Tracking strategy in an entrepreneurial firm", Academy of Management Journal, Vol. 25.

Moore, G.A. (1991), Crossing the Chasm, Harpers Collins, New York, NY.

Mootee, I. (1998), Escape Velocity, Knowledge Capital Publishing, NY.

Monroe, K.B. (1973), "Buyers' subjective perceptions of price", Journal of Marketing Research, Vol. 10.

Monroe, K.B. (1990), Pricing: Making Profitable Decisions, 2nd ed., McGraw-Hill, New York, NY.

O'Connor, L. (1993), "Energizing the batteries for electric cars", Mechanical Engineering, Vol. 115.

Oren, S.S. and Schwartz, R.G. (1988), "Diffusion of new products in risk-sensitive markets", Journal of Forecasting, Vol. 7.

Ozanne, J.L., Brucks, M. and Grewal, D. (1992), "A study of information search behavior during the categorization of new product", Journal of Consumer Research, Vol. 18.

Payton, T.H. (1995), "The electric car – some problems of driver attitudes and product fit", Journal of the Marketing Research Society, Vol. 30.

Porac, J., Thomas, H. and Emme, B. (1987), "Knowing the competition", in Johnson, G. (Ed.), Business Strategy and Retailing, J. Wiley, Chichester.

Porter, M.E. (1980), Competitive Strategy. Technique for Analyzing Industries and Competitors. The Free Press, New York.

Porter, M.E. (1987), From Competitive Advantage to Corporate Strategy. Harvard Business Review. March.

Quelch, J.A. and Harding, D. (1996), "Brands versus private labels: fighting to win", Harvard Business Review, Vol. 74.

Ries, A. and Trout, J. (1986), Marketing Warfare, McGraw Hill, New York, NY.

Rogers, E.M. (1983), Diffusion of Innovations, The Free Press, New York, NY.

Scammon, D.L. (1977), "Information overload and consumers", Journal of Consumer Research, Vol. 4.

Shimp, T.A. and Bearden, W.O. (1982), "Warranty and other extrinsic cue effects on consumers' risk perceptions", Journal of Consumer Research, Vol. 9.

Schwenk, C. (1988), The Essence of Strategic Decision Making, Lexington Books, Lexington, MA.

Solomon, M.R. (1986), "The missing link: surrogate consumers in the marketing chain", Journal of Marketing, Vol. 50.

Sternberg, R.J. (1986), "Inside intelligence", American Scientist, Vol. 74.

Sujan, M. (1985), "Consumer knowledge: effects on evaluation strategies mediating consumer judgments", Journal of Consumer Research, Vol. 12.

Steiner, G. and Miner, J. (1977), Management Policy and Strategy, Macmillan, New York, NY.

Stobart, P. (1994), Brand Power, Macmillan, Basingstoke.

Tidd, J. (1995), "Development of novel products through intraorganizational and interorganizational networks: the case of home automation", Journal of Product Innovation Management, Vol. 12.

Urban, G.L., Weinberg, B.D. and Hauser, J.R. (1996), "Premarket forecasting of really-new products", Journal of Marketing, Vol. 60.

Visnic, B. (1996), "GM's big event", Ward's Auto World, Vol. 32.

Wernerfelt, B. (1991), "Brand loyalty and market equilibrium", Marketing Science, Vol. 10.

Wendell R. Smith (1956), "Product Differentiation and Segmentation as Alternative Marketing Strategies". Journal of Marketing, July

INDEX